Working in Teaching

Working in Teaching

Alan Newland, newteachersblog.wordpress.com

Working in Teaching

This first edition published in 2014 by Trotman Education, an imprint of Crimson Publishing Ltd, The Tramshed, Walcot Street, Bath BA1 5BB

© Trotman Education 2014

Author: Alan Newland

The right of Alan Newland to be identified as the author of this work has been asserted by him in accordance with the Copyright, Designs and Patents Act 1988.

British Library Cataloguing in Publication Data
A catalogue record for this book is available from the British Library

ISBN 978 0 9568350 2 4

Typeset by IDSUK (DataConnection) Ltd
Printed and bound in Malta by Gutenberg Press Ltd, Malta

Contents

Contents

About the author

Alan Newland has worked in education for more than 34 years – as a teacher, lecturer in teacher training, head teacher and adviser at the Department for Education and the General Teaching Council. He continues to present engaging and thought-provoking lectures on ethics and professional values to thousands of students and trainees about to graduate as teachers every year. He also runs an award-winning blog and social network for new teachers, newteacherstalk. He is a fellow of the Royal Society of Arts and lives in north London.

Acknowledgements

My sincere and heartfelt thanks go to all those students, trainees, teachers, tutors and lecturers who interrupted their very busy lives to help me write this book. In no particular order, they are:

Laura Harris, Clare Dempsey, Lauren Kavanagh, Tommy Jordan, Andreana Panayi, Mohammed Wassiq, Clare Gordge, Anjuman Chaudhary, Rosie Marsh, Charlotte Hopperton, Kirsty Anderson-Dawes, Salma Alam-Naylor, Warren Valentine, Rachael Holmes, Louise Foster, William Oulton, Sarah Colyer, Catriona Meecham, Guy Lochhead, Leanne Buckley, Amanda Harvey, Cheryl Letts, Melissa Fearon, Laura Bellars, Anthea Meek, Ben Shields, Claire Skilbeck, Julia Pavey, Anthony Parker, Veronica Towers, Philippa Briscoe, Janine Rumble, Katrina Chambers, Stephanie Firth, Mark Crossley, Chris Hildrew, Laura McInerney, Colin Forster, Chris King, Kenny Pieper, Samantha George, K.V. Lapsley, G. Hartland, Susan Wood, Sarah Flanagan, Fearghal Kelly, Bryn Harrison, Keither Parker, Nick Hood, Paul Smalley, Jacqui Vaughan, Janet Blake, Darren Barton, Andy Howes, Jonathon Glazzard, Neil Stanley, Sue Skyrme, Dominic Coughlan, Adrian Copping, Pete Yeomans, Salliann Coleman.

Introduction

It's great that you're thinking of becoming a teacher. It is *the* profession that is fundamental to how society conveys not only the skills and knowledge it deems essential, but its values too. Can you think of any other significant job, trade or profession that doesn't rely on teaching to be what it is? Surely that makes it one of the most important jobs in the world.

Apart from being a very significant thing to do, it also has the benefit of being great fun, thoroughly inspiring, and a source for learning new things every day. As a teacher, you will never have to ask yourself why you are getting out of bed in the morning. Not only that, but these days it's not badly paid either.

That's not to say that it doesn't have significant challenges of course – because it does. But teaching children of any age or ability in any part of the UK, whether in an idyllic rural village or on a tough inner-city council estate, can be a richly rewarding and life-enhancing experience. It is a job that you not only look forward to going to every day, but also one you can look back on with a deep sense of satisfaction once your career has ended.

Being a teacher is a vital role in society. Throughout history, all successful civilisations have invested huge importance in teachers as central figures with influence and authority (which is why in other societies they have names such as rabbi, guru and professor). Teachers are key to the way a society passes on its knowledge, culture and values from one generation to another.

These days, there is a widening variety of ways to become a teacher. The traditional routes of training either as an undergraduate or postgraduate on a university- or college-based course are still by far the most popular, but opportunities to train on the job are broadening through employment-based routes, which can provide a salary while you qualify. Almost all new teachers are graduates, but there are still ways into teaching that do not require a degree, particularly if you have relevant experience, such as a background in commerce, industry or the military, and the appropriate aptitudes to go with it, such as business, technical or scientific skills and knowledge.

Introduction

As this book will explain, you will need to be careful about choosing which route is right for you because the way you are trained and the support you receive lays the foundations of your skills as a teacher. The way your needs are met through a particular training course will directly affect the confidence you develop in taking a class of your own for the first time.

One of the great attractions of a career in teaching is the enormous variety it provides. As a primary school teacher, you may have the same 30 children every day for a year, but you are teaching them almost everything they learn in school: English, maths, science, computing, history, geography, art, sports, PE and drama, and maybe even music or a foreign language. Don't be daunted by that. You'll find it great fun learning new things in preparation for the role. What you can't teach yourself or haven't been trained for, you'll find plenty of help in; there are increasing numbers of specialists employed to train teachers in specialisms such as music, PE and foreign language as a result of government-funded schemes in these subjects.

In secondary schools, while you might be a specialist in one or two subjects such as biology and chemistry, you may well be teaching general science to a lively and enquiring group of 12-year-olds at the start of the day and A level biology to a group of studious 17-year-olds by the end of it. Not only that, you may get involved in running a school sports team, organising a dance or drama club, a ski trip or an adventure holiday.

The skills teachers acquire, even in their first year or two, are often highly transferrable. Teachers soon become extremely adept at managing time, resources and particularly people. Indeed, one of teaching's key skills is the ability to motivate, coach and inspire others, and because communication skills are so central to the job, teachers usually learn to be good team players too.

This book is intended to give a realistic view of teaching, so as well as describing teaching as inspiring and life-enhancing, it won't gloss over the very real challenges and issues teachers face – especially new teachers. The first few years in the job can be particularly difficult as you face balancing the demands of planning, preparing and marking – and all the others things you have to do as a teacher – with maintaining the kind of social and family life that will keep you grounded and sane.

This book will look at the crucial first year or two in the job and discuss how you can make sure that both your professional and your personal needs are being met. It will consider the options available to you once you are in the profession – such as the implications of taking on further responsibility or specialising in particular areas – as well as the costs and benefits of doing things such as a master's degree or even a doctorate.

It will also look at what you can realistically expect from daily life in the classroom and how you can access support and advice to sustain, motivate and move you forward. Even during your first year, perhaps especially during it, your own professional learning will be key – not just in keeping up to date with the latest methods and techniques of teaching, but as a way of motivating you and giving you a sense of direction for the future. You will want to *learn* as much as you'll want to teach. So this book will also explore aspects of your own professional learning at the beginning of your career.

There are more than 30,000 schools in the UK and well over half a million teachers, so the potential for promotion and advancement is enormous. But it varies considerably from region to region, largely for reasons of scale – the size and number of schools in a particular area – and mobility. Clearly, finding work in rural, sparsely populated areas of the UK may be a challenge, but it's not hopeless if you have particularly sought-after skills or aptitudes to offer. Some conurbations and inner-city areas have a high turnover rate, whereas others don't; and while local circumstances vary, the trend is clear. These days, people want to be teachers, and so the competition to get on training courses, and to get jobs at the end of them, is continuing to increase.

Many people choose to become teachers because they are ardent and enthusiastic learners themselves. Teaching is a great job for those who have a passion they want to pass on to others, such as a love of music, literature, mathematics, science or the arts. Teaching provides a lifelong opportunity to immerse yourself in the very things that you find wonderful, stimulating and inspiring. Watching young people learn and discover new things for the first time can fill you with a great sense of satisfaction and gratitude. Those "light-bulb moments", when children suddenly realise they understand something new and shout out with uncontained excitement "I get it now!", are a regular occurrence for most teachers.

Introduction

So if you think you might like working with young people, watching them learn, develop and grow, or you have a passion you want others to discover, or you love learning new things yourself and want to develop new skills through some serious responsibility – teaching may just be the job for you!

PART 1
Heading into teaching

1

Why teaching?

Let's start with "Why?"

People choose careers for a variety of reasons, and those reasons can range from the idealistic, philosophical and even political to the more pragmatic, financial and downright practical. There are lots of brilliant teachers out there who went into teaching because of the long summer holidays and the family-friendly hours. As long as you develop into a brilliant teacher, your initial motivation, however self-serving, might turn out to be a happy accident. (But if the long summer holidays are your only motivation, you may soon find that they are not nearly long enough.)

Most of us find that our ability and aptitude to do a job is strongly linked to motivation. You will need to examine yours, probably more deeply than you would otherwise, when it comes to deciding whether teaching is for you. Idealism can be a strong initial driver. It may well sustain you through the challenging first few years, and your later career, too. But don't be embarrassed by admitting that pragmatic and practical reasons have also informed your decision. Having your reasons, whatever they are, as *clear, objective* and *explicit* will help you maintain your focus.

You will of course be asked about this at the application and interview stages for teacher training, so it's important to think through the reasons and associated issues beforehand. Let's spend a few minutes doing just that now.

What's my motivation?

Try this little exercise. It aims to assess what might motivate you to be a teacher. Give yourself points between 0 and 10 for each of the statements: 0 if it makes you think "That's not me at all!", up to 10 if you think "That's me to a tee!".

There's no psychoanalysis at the end. Just take a look at your results and draw your own conclusions.

I love children and want to work with them.	0 1 2 3 4 5 6 7 8 9 10
I have a passion for a subject and want others to love it too.	0 1 2 3 4 5 6 7 8 9 10
I love learning new things.	0 1 2 3 4 5 6 7 8 9 10
I want to inspire others to fulfil their potential.	0 1 2 3 4 5 6 7 8 9 10
I want to give something back to society.	0 1 2 3 4 5 6 7 8 9 10
I need to provide and care for a family.	0 1 2 3 4 5 6 7 8 9 10
School hours and holidays appeal to my lifestyle.	0 1 2 3 4 5 6 7 8 9 10
Teaching is a tradition in our family.	0 1 2 3 4 5 6 7 8 9 10
I am bored and disillusioned with my current job.	0 1 2 3 4 5 6 7 8 9 10
I want to do something meaningful with my life.	0 1 2 3 4 5 6 7 8 9 10
I want a job with complex responsibilities.	0 1 2 3 4 5 6 7 8 9 10
High levels of accountability don't concern me.	0 1 2 3 4 5 6 7 8 9 10
I want a job with a regular salary every month.	0 1 2 3 4 5 6 7 8 9 10
I want a job with a good pension in 40 years' time.	0 1 2 3 4 5 6 7 8 9 10
I want a job where I am unlikely to be made redundant.	0 1 2 3 4 5 6 7 8 9 10
I want a job that is very challenging, even stressful at times.	0 1 2 3 4 5 6 7 8 9 10
I want a job with a great deal of variety.	0 1 2 3 4 5 6 7 8 9 10

Most people who have decided to become teachers will tell you their reasons correspond to a combination of these statements, not just one. Kirsty Anderson Dawes, a secondary geography Postgraduate Certificate in Education (PGCE) student currently at Nottingham University, is one of them.

> "My motivation for teaching comes from a love of my subject. Despite the cliché, I want to translate that excitement to young people and help them appreciate and understand the world in which they live. Alongside that, I want to contribute to instilling a sense of self and confidence into students, allowing them to fulfil their own potential.

> "For me, the beauty of teaching is that no two days are ever the same. No matter how experienced you are as a teacher, there will always be challenges and things you never expected to encounter. In addition, becoming a teacher has lots of opportunities for progression; not only as head of department but other opportunities within education.

> "I like the pace of the school day alongside the opportunity to work with so many different people. Unlike other jobs, there will always be a need for teachers and education, possibly even more so in the future. As a geographer, I appreciate the lengths of the holidays so I can travel."

Kirsty's reasons are summed up quite clearly as a combination of factors including personal, even selfish, ones such as the time to pursue her enjoyment of travel. You will meet teachers who are very idealistic about what they do (and some who have become terribly cynical ...). You'll feel the pressure to rehearse some high-sounding and idealistic reasons for wanting to be a teacher, especially when you go for interview at a training provider. But having a passion for a subject is as good a reason as any and should be highlighted, especially if you are thinking of becoming a secondary teacher.

Warren Valentine is one such person. He did a history PGCE in London last year:

> "I had fully thrown myself into my history degree. I loved it enormously and was very sad when it ended. I did not really

> want to leave history behind. It is something I love, enjoy and have proved reasonably good at — I got a first in my degree. I started a PGCE immediately after my degree. The professor I truly admired at university could refer to any period in any context. I want to be like that and move on and complete an MA in History. "

A love of a subject can be one thing when you are the learner, but, of course, it might be quite a different thing when you have to teach the subject and present that knowledge in a way that makes it appealing and digestible for others. For some people, this is the quickest way to get fed up with something they once loved. Loving fish and chips doesn't mean you'll love running a fish and chip shop, or even be good at it — so be careful.

Not everyone who has gone on to a successful teaching career came to it knowing that it was something they always wanted to do. Many people find a career they have become passionate about simply by trying it out, to see whether their perception is consistent with experience. Others admit coming across an opportunity almost by accident and discovering an unknown aptitude, or finding themselves needing to take a job out of temporary necessity only to find it provided longer-term gains and satisfactions. The reality is that many us fall into a job and then discover its virtues.

Amanda Harvey is one such person. She is doing a BA in Primary Education with an option to acquire Qualified Teacher Status:

> "I worked for eight years as a professional actress and when not performing, I fell into doing teaching workshops and school clubs specialising in drama and music to earn some money. Then I had my daughter and acting lost its appeal, so I decided to formalise the work I was doing with children and young people and worked as an unqualified teacher. I discovered I enjoyed it. "

Another person who fell into it was Lubna:

> "I fell into teaching out of necessity to pay the bills — that seems to be the default for many music graduates in my

experience. I was working as a freelance music teacher in a variety of guises and began to really enjoy it, so decided to take my work to the next level and train to become a qualified teacher. I guess the security of a regular salary attracted me on some level — the politics of the profession certainly didn't. However, the possibility that I could make a difference to other people's lives inspired me. I've always been a musician and I have never been able to imagine doing something else and so the idea of being involved in music-making all my working week was a very exciting prospect."

Spending the working week doing what you love and being paid for it is most people's idea of a dream job, which is why many teachers genuinely feel they have the best job in the world. But occasionally even heady idealism will be tempered by the odd negative experience or false start. Philippa Briscoe qualified last year and found that her initial experience of teaching was less than ideal:

"I grew up always wanting to be a teacher, but then while on work experience at university I tried it a few times and became completely disillusioned. Coming from a grammar school I had no idea how to inspire students in a failing school, and at that point walked away from the idea of teaching as a career.

"After a few years working in event management, I decided that I wanted to do something more meaningful and significant with my life. Having used English in practical ways within marketing and communications, I decided to try teaching again and pass on the benefit of my 'real-world' uses of the subject to others."

False starts and self-doubts are very typical when beginning a new career and young people, especially where they are lacking other reference points, will be plagued by mini-crises, wondering whether they have done the right thing. Sometimes people find that they have a better perspective after a period of reflection doing something else. Leanne Buckley always thought she had ambitions to be a PE teacher, but the route she has taken into teaching wasn't as straightforward as she had imagined:

"As a child it was always my ambition to become a PE teacher, until I started a sports science degree. After six months of doing that I decided teaching wasn't for me. I lacked confidence and self-belief, and changed my degree to study social psychology. This opened up lots of doors, and though I still remained interested in sport, I realised it was more of a hobby than a career choice. Then after leaving university, I spent five years working in California as the aquatics director for a charity for people who are blind or visually impaired. On my return to the UK, I got a job supporting people with learning difficulties and disabilities. Within 12 months I found I was covering classes, developing strategies, conducting support assessments and so on, and I was being developed both personally and professionally.

"Then last year I had a light-bulb moment where I had been covering a tutor on long-term absence and thought to myself, 'I can do this!' So I went home that evening and applied for a place on a PGCE. The break from finishing my degree to starting my PGCE enabled me to gain real-life, relevant experience and enhanced my personal development in a way that isn't always possible when you are in continuous education. "

So, while some people fall into teaching more by accident than design, others talk about the "light-bulb moments" when they realised they had a talent for showing others how things can be different. For some, the discovery comes only as a result of having to do something to pay the bills. None of these reasons has a moral superiority over any other, so there's no need to think that your decision has to be grounded in philosophy any more than it does pragmatism. Once you are teaching well and enjoying the feeling, you will soon be able to find reasons to justify it to yourself and those around you, if you need to.

These days, you can sample teaching by doing work experience or volunteering. Indeed, you will probably have to – in order to meet the ever-growing entry requirements, teacher-training providers are demanding that candidates complete a period of school experience even before applying for a training position.

Many people discover, quite by accident, that they have a particular aptitude in demonstrating or modelling a skill or creating a problem-solving opportunity. Tom

Jordan is now a business studies teacher, but his journey into teaching started by helping children tie their shoes at a US summer camp:

> "While at university I spent one summer working in a summer camp in New York. I found it a real challenge, but the main source of my enjoyment and motivation was the problem-solving element to it. I was in charge of a group of 6–10-year-olds who all had trouble tying their shoelaces. Another counsellor and I created a range of small cardboard shoes to give to the children to practice during their free time in the day. I watched as children picked up the skill miraculously. The elation and sense of pride they gained was so exciting to see that it was the trigger for me to want to go into teaching."

As with many other careers and professions, the love of a particular job can be passed on from one generation to another and many teachers will tell you they come from a family of teachers. Family traditions can be a powerful influence on career choice. Many people inherit a strong sense of public service, dedication and even a passion for a particular profession, craft or trade from their parents or members of their extended family. While you must be wary of the weight of expectation and the possible constraining implications of living up to tradition, it can also provide a strong sense of direction and a great pool of support and advice, especially when the challenges and the inevitable stresses and strains begin to emerge.

Charlotte Hopperton, a new geography teacher, is a good example of this:

> "My biggest motivation was my family, as they have all worked in some form of public service. My father was a paramedic and my mother a learning support assistant. Both my aunt and uncle are in the medical profession as a community nurse and a GP. My father always told me: 'Go out and do something. Don't sit there watching the world pass you by.'"

Teaching is a job with regular hours, a decent salary, relatively family-friendly working hours and a reasonable degree of job security, so for many people the relative stability and security are key issues. These can be powerful drivers, especially if you are thinking of having a family or already have one that you need to provide for. Mohammed Wassiq is a music teacher, and he was very clear about this when making his decision:

> *"My main motivation for choosing to teach was to have a stable career, pension and security for my family. I was at a point where I was freelancing as a lecturer and though the money was good, I was being drip-fed work that was not always regular."*

While teaching still retains a relatively high degree of job security and stability, things are beginning to change. The pressures on schools and the individual performance of teachers have changed the landscape in the last decade or two. Teachers can now find themselves the subject of performance reviews that sometimes lead to competence procedures and even dismissal. Redundancy, while still relatively rare, was once completely unheard of in teaching. Not any longer. These days, schools are closing down where the demographic profile of an area changes substantially. Many schools are changing their status – becoming academies or "free schools" – and imposing new and revised contracts on teachers, quite separate from the national agreements that were once standard across the board.

A recurring theme for many teachers, however, including many of those interviewed for this book, is the role an inspirational teacher from their own school days played in their decision to become a teacher themselves. This is certainly true for Laura Bellars, currently training to be a primary teacher on an undergraduate route:

> *"One of my own primary teachers inspired me to become a teacher. Her passion for learning is something I have never forgotten. She always made time for every child and provided constant support to ensure we made progress. I am finding that primary teaching is a very rewarding job. During my teaching placements, when I see that children understand something as a result of my teaching I get a great feeling of pride. Having the opportunity to inspire a love of learning and making a difference in children's lives is something I am really looking forward to."*

Profile: University of Hertfordshire

Based In Hatfield and surrounded by open space, but just a 20-minute train ride from central London, the School of Education at the University of Hertfordshire is a well-established provider of initial teacher education at undergraduate and postgraduate level.

It has expertise in secondary, primary and early years education that goes back many years, from its proud beginning as the first emergency women's teacher-training college in the UK, opened by R. A. Butler, Minister of Education, in 1945.

The School of Education is committed to developing excellence and confidence in teaching, learning and professional practice. It offers a wide range of programmes for individuals and exciting ways of working with partner organisations. The School works in close partnership with almost 700 primary and secondary schools across 12 local authorities. This partnership offers students the opportunity to develop their understanding of teaching and their classroom practice together, for example by learning about special educational needs, phonics or English as a second language, both at the university and through dedicated school visits in addition to their school-based training.

The School of Education is proud of its record of supporting students through their training. The most recent OFSTED report, in 2011, said that a particular feature of the School's work was: "... the excellent quality of personal, professional and academic support for trainees on all programmes, to ensure their well-being and to enable them to demonstrate highly professional attributes".

OFSTED also commented on the School's enviable record for employability, which is built on both quality of training and the strong partnership with local schools. Every year, hundreds of new teachers from Hertfordshire take up their first teaching posts. Typically, over 90% of students have a teaching job within six months.

Sal Jarvis, Dean of the School of Education said: "The people in the School of Education are one of its greatest strengths. We have students who are self-motivated, reflective, professional and absolutely committed to supporting their pupils' learning. Our student teachers praise their university tutors for being so enthusiastic about their teaching and committed to their students.

"Studying in the School of Education at the University of Hertfordshire you'll have plenty of interactive, small-group work as well as lectures from experienced teachers. You'll work in schools alongside teachers who can help you develop your own excellent teaching. On campus you'll have first-class teaching, sporting and leisure facilities. Most of all, however, you'll make friends for life who'll be your support network throughout your teaching career. The School of Education at the University of Hertfordshire is a great place to train."

Case study

The PGCE primary programme allows students to develop the skills required by primary teachers to teach the full range of National Curriculum subjects, with a strong emphasis on English and mathematics, and to develop specific expertise for making a distinctive contribution to primary practice.

It is an intensive course that requires a good deal of physical and emotional resilience to complete successfully. Here's what last year's students had to say after they came back from their first placement:

"There are moments of panic and stress, but the day a child looks at you and says, 'I get it now!' will make all the hard times and the hard work completely worth it."

"It is amazing how much you learn so quickly, both at uni and on placement. It doesn't get any easier, though, and there is always something new to learn."

"Three hours' sleep and 21 hours of work a day. Worth it, though, to captivate 35 fresh minds!"

"Over the past few weeks of placement I feel I have made a difference to other people's lives. We were always told this was part of being a teacher, but doing this in practice is a feeling like no other."

What do I have to offer?

Part of the process for deciding on any career path is the assessment you (and others) will make about the aptitude, talent and ability you have to do the job. In other words, what do *you* have to offer?

These days, there are fairly rigorous interview and selection procedures, both for a place on a training course and for a job in a school. Both will ask the question: "What do you have to offer?" and test the evidence you provide. The better you know your own strengths and can articulate them, the better chance you will have of understanding whether those strengths are a suitable match for teaching. Once you have an understanding of that, you can prepare a successful application to train as a teacher and secure your first appointment.

See how you get on with this short series of exercises intended to help you identify your strengths and weaknesses.

Exercise one

Assess the following aptitudes, skills and abilities. Remember, this exercise is for you, so you need to be honest with yourself. All of the statements below describe the attributes of good teaching. It may help you identify which attributes you have in abundance and which you lack, or need to work on, once you have made the decision to become a teacher. You won't be expected to have them all well honed and polished by the time you interview for a course, let alone starting your first job. But knowing your strengths and weaknesses, even at this stage, will help you decide if teaching is really for you. Remember to be realistic – thinking of yourself in superlatives won't help.

Mark these up where 0 is a weakness and 10 is a strength. There's no analysis or counting up of totals at the end; just take a look at the pattern of your grades. Keep it private – you are more likely to be truthful that way.

Afterwards, reflect. Did this tell you anything about yourself? Will this exercise help you tell the story of yourself to others?

I am well organised in my own affairs.	0 1 2 3 4 5 6 7 8 9 10
I can organise other people.	0 1 2 3 4 5 6 7 8 9 10
I'm good at managing time.	0 1 2 3 4 5 6 7 8 9 10
I'm punctual.	0 1 2 3 4 5 6 7 8 9 10
I prepare well for tasks and meetings.	0 1 2 3 4 5 6 7 8 9 10
I enjoy working in teams.	0 1 2 3 4 5 6 7 8 9 10
I enjoy working independently.	0 1 2 3 4 5 6 7 8 9 10
I'm a good communicator.	0 1 2 3 4 5 6 7 8 9 10
I can speak confidently to large audiences.	0 1 2 3 4 5 6 7 8 9 10
I can handle pressure.	0 1 2 3 4 5 6 7 8 9 10
I can handle stress.	0 1 2 3 4 5 6 7 8 9 10
I see things from other people's point of view.	0 1 2 3 4 5 6 7 8 9 10
I can negotiate.	0 1 2 3 4 5 6 7 8 9 10
I give clear directions.	0 1 2 3 4 5 6 7 8 9 10
I am assertive.	0 1 2 3 4 5 6 7 8 9 10

I have a good sense of humour.	0 1 2 3 4 5 6 7 8 9 10
I'm a good listener.	0 1 2 3 4 5 6 7 8 9 10
I am patient.	0 1 2 3 4 5 6 7 8 9 10
I am positive when problems arise.	0 1 2 3 4 5 6 7 8 9 10
I am still positive with people who appear negative.	0 1 2 3 4 5 6 7 8 9 10
I am creative.	0 1 2 3 4 5 6 7 8 9 10
I understand the need for theory.	0 1 2 3 4 5 6 7 8 9 10
I keep my head in a crisis.	0 1 2 3 4 5 6 7 8 9 10
I can empathise with people from different social backgrounds.	0 1 2 3 4 5 6 7 8 9 10
I can relate to people from different ethnic groups.	0 1 2 3 4 5 6 7 8 9 10
I respect the religious beliefs of others.	0 1 2 3 4 5 6 7 8 9 10
I can get on with anybody, even when they don't like me.	0 1 2 3 4 5 6 7 8 9 10
I am reflective and thoughtful.	0 1 2 3 4 5 6 7 8 9 10
I have a thick skin.	0 1 2 3 4 5 6 7 8 9 10
I am friendly and approachable.	0 1 2 3 4 5 6 7 8 9 10

Exercise two

Here's another useful little exercise to do off the back of the previous one. Again, it will be very useful in telling you whether you are a good match for teaching, as well as excellent preparation for your interview. Write a list of experiences and skills you have that you think are relevant to teaching. Some questions are given below to help you.

- Do you have any musical, technical, computational or language skills?

- Do you have any sports or hobbies that you are enthusiastic or passionate about?

- Do you have crafts and creative skills that you enjoy or have developed to a reasonably high level?

- Have you ever been in positions of responsibility – for example, were you a school prefect or team captain, secretary or treasurer of a club or society at university?
- Have you had a previous career in industry, commerce, technology or public service, even for a short time?
- Have you ever managed other people, budgets or resources, such as being a supervisor in a shop or responsible for opening and closing premises?

Exercise three

The next exercise is important, as all training providers and teaching jobs require a supporting statement. Turn your list from exercise two into a narrative of yourself that comprises a personal statement of what you have to offer. Keep it to two sides of A4, or about 750–800 words. If you go over that word limit on your first draft, edit it down. Select the highlights from your list, giving examples (if you can) of what you did and how you did it. If possible, point to any tangible achievement or outcome. Here are a couple of examples.

Let's say in your list you wrote "I can play the guitar". In your statement, explain how you came to learn it and how long you have been playing ("I started playing the guitar from the age of seven when I bought one from a music shop with my birthday savings . . ."), where and when you play it ("I play occasionally at pubs, parties and sing-songs with my family on holidays . . .") and what level of competence you have achieved ("I recently passed Grade 4 of the Registry of Guitar Tutors exams . . .").

Try to turn your statement into one that reflects a little of your character and personality, as well the skill or expertise you have to offer. Here is another example:

"At university, I created and managed a website for the university sailing club. I have Java, MySQL and Drupal coding skills, and like teaching others how to program. The website for the sailing club improved the way we could engage members in activities as the online community element of it helped us organise race meetings, club volunteers and attract new members."

Exercise four

Send an email to eight to 10 people who know you really well. These should be close friends, long-term colleagues you can trust and family members you like. Ask them to state, frankly and honestly, the one or two most apparent and outstanding qualities you have. One-word answers will do, as the exercise should be done without much thought. But don't tell them it's because you are thinking of becoming a teacher — say it's an exercise for a job. This should give you an insight into how others perceive your strengths, and build up your confidence.

Don't be tempted to include in your application letters and supporting statements cheesy lines such as: "My friends tell me I'm this . . . that . . . and the other . . .". That is not the way to use this information. Simply let it inform your judgement about what to include and emphasise about your own qualities.

Whatever they are, you've made a start in consciously considering the reasons you want to be a teacher and what you think you bring to the table. Making such an important decision deserves time and thought, particularly as it's the kind of job where you have to take on not only an enormous amount of skills and knowledge in a short time, but also accommodate the way others perceive you. That has implications for your self-image and identity, particularly as you will be seen as a professional.

This brings us to the next issue: you, becoming a professional person.

Is teaching a profession?

Some people are attracted to teaching because it is a "profession" with a corresponding status in the eyes of the public. Teaching has always been an occupation highly regarded by the general public, alongside nursing and medicine. But the picture is complicated.

Three decades ago, teaching appeared low on the list of the top 20 graduate career choices. Now it is regularly in the top three or four. You may think that's because of the current economic recession. It's not. For the last 12–15 years, teacher-training courses have been heavily oversubscribed, with most training providers receiving 10 times as many applicants as there are places available.

In recent years, central government has played its part in making teaching a more attractive profession by virtue of better pay, professional development opportunities and investment in school buildings. There have been financial incentives too, such as starting bonuses to attract graduates in subjects such as maths, chemistry and physics that suffer from a shortage of teachers. There have also been innovative schemes to attract top graduates from elite universities, such as Teach First.

It doesn't stop with young new graduates either. The biggest single group of people coming into teaching these days are career-changers – those people who have worked elsewhere but decided to seek a different kind of job satisfaction than perhaps mere financial reward.

Twenty years ago, there were advertising campaigns across Europe, Australia, New Zealand and the Caribbean to recruit teachers for the UK education system because shortages were so acute, especially in inner cities. These days, by contrast, people want to be teachers. That means more intense competition just to get on a training course, and that's even before you qualify and start looking for your first teaching post. Competition increases in some parts of the country where there is low teacher mobility from school to school and fewer jobs become available.

Entering an intensely competitive arena might not feel good if you are thinking about teaching, but just look at the bigger picture. For the first time in decades the best and brightest graduates and career-changers are getting into teaching. That can only be good for the education of children, for schools themselves and for the country and our society at large. Greater competition has led to higher standards of entrants, and should ultimately lead to enhanced professional status and public regard.

But what is a profession?

This is an important question and you need to think about it. Is teaching regarded in the same way as other established professions such as medicine, law, nursing and accountancy? Or is it largely a skills-based trade or craft, as are the roles of electrician, joiner, plumber or hairdresser?

This is a complex area, but it's worth spending a moment considering these questions because there are problems surrounding the reasons why people are motivated to be a "professional" in the first place.

The questions and the debate around teaching are not new. Some people, including teachers and leading politicians, do not to refer to it as a "profession" but more often as a "craft". Even academics at universities have argued about whether teaching displays all the characteristics of an established profession. Some have concluded that it does not.

Before we go any further, let's take a little time to jot down a list of characteristics that you think define a profession. This is important, and we'll understand why shortly. This is a good activity to help you prepare for your teacher-training interview, too.

Exercise five

What is a profession?

Write a list of six or seven characteristics that you think define a "profession".

. . .

How did you get on? What was on your list?

You may have listed things such as the following.

- You need a high standard of education to train or enter a profession.

- You need professional qualifications to qualify, such as an LLB or PGCE, and specialist training related to it.

- There have to be nationally recognised standards so you can practise your profession from Cornwall to Cumbria.

- Members of the profession adhere to professional codes of competence, conduct and practice.

- Members must register with a professional body or association, such as the General Medical Council or the Institution of Civil Engineers.

- Members commit to career-long continuing professional development (CPD).

- Members enter a community of shared values and expectations, drawing on or contributing to a body of knowledge, informed by research, theory and practice.

- A career structure exists, with clear opportunities to advance through additional responsibility, specialisation or seniority.

- The public expects dedicated and committed service.

- Members are trusted to take on complex and weighty responsibilities and make judgements in the best interests of their clients.

- Members are highly accountable for their actions to a wide range of stakeholders, which can include the government, inspection bodies, employers, local authorities, trustees, governors or clients.

- Members of professions are sometimes considered or expected to be role models.

Of course, this is by no means a definitive list. What constitutes a "profession" is open to wide interpretation, especially these days when the definition is itself a matter of some debate.

But the exercise raises enough questions for you to think about some of the issues inherent in a values-led profession such as teaching. For example, there are some clear implications about how your personal identity will be challenged to accommodate changes in the way you will be perceived by others, such as the expectation that you will behave and be perceived as a role model for young people.

There is another area that bears on your personal life. In teaching, you will be challenged by the boundaries between your personal and professional life in ways that few other jobs do. Does the public expect the same things from an electrician, plumber, hairdresser or car mechanic as they do from a doctor, lawyer, nurse or teacher?

What used to be called "trades" are increasingly professionalising and taking on the characteristics of established professions, such as professional bodies and associations, codes of conduct and practice, entry qualifications, standards and so on. You may well have met builders or car mechanics who fulfil many or all of the criteria for being a member of a profession. Many certainly have a passion for what they do and are dedicated to customer satisfaction and quality of service.

For example, you may come across some excellent car mechanics who have no formal qualifications in the field. Does that matter? Perhaps all you are concerned about is that they do a good job servicing your car at a reasonable price.

But society requires a different standard for those wishing to practise medicine, law, nursing or teaching. For example, most people want to know that the person standing in front of their child is trained and qualified to do that job to the high standard we all expect.

Your car mechanic may be a very nice person, but usually you'll have no idea about their background. Maybe all you are concerned about is what is relevant to the job you are asking them to do. Surely the issue is whether they do a good job on your car at a reasonable price, and whatever they have done in their private life is of no relevance or concern.

But suppose your child's teacher had a criminal conviction? That may be an aspect of their background you would need to be reassured about before feeling comfortable that your child was being taught by an appropriate, responsible person. This is not to say that society shouldn't forgive foolish mistakes – perhaps made in a misspent youth – but nevertheless, most parents would want, at the very least, some reassurance that their child's teacher was no longer making mistakes of that nature!

Many teaching applicants have minor convictions or cautions for misdemeanours. Don't worry too much if you have. Very few people are barred from applying for teaching for minor offences, although we'll deal in more detail with the issue of offences and checks later.

But most people simply expect a different standard of personal behaviour from those in established professions. The reasons are probably related to the public's expectations regarding concepts such as trust, responsibility, duty of care or being a role model.

Whatever the reasons, those expectations exist and are real. Let's explore this a little more, particularly in relation to you.

Professional expectations; private lives

As you enter teaching, you will sense the expectations of your colleagues, children and their parents, among others. You may sometimes find it a little constraining or unreasonable and it may even make you feel claustrophobic. Try not to respond in this way. You have a right to a private life, and you'll probably want to have a reasonably active social life too. Although you are expected to be a role model, you are not expected to be an angel. Not even as a teacher.

You may legitimately take the view that if you are good teacher, why is it anyone else's business what you do in your private life? This is a very important question.

Exercise six

Think about the following scenarios and decide where you stand on each.

If you are good teacher, does it matter whether you:

- regularly get drunk in pubs or clubs at weekends?

- use dance drugs in a nightclub or recreational drugs in the privacy of your own home?

- regularly exceed the speed limit?

- download adult pornography using your home computer?

- engage in flirtatious and sexualised banter with colleagues?

- become active in an extreme political party?

Go away and discuss these with a friend, a trusted colleague or a member of your family. Think about them carefully. No one-word answers will do for this.

These scenarios bring in to focus how teaching is a values-led profession, and that you will need to make cautious judgements about how you manage the boundaries between your professional and personal life. Managing and protecting your public reputation will be more important to you now that, as a teacher, even aspects of your personal behaviour may come under scrutiny. People may make judgements about you – even judgements based on their standards of morality – that they have no right to make. The problem is, whether you like it or not, those judgements may impinge on you and on the way you are perceived by others, particularly the children and young people you will work with and their parents. Their perceptions could make your working life much more difficult to manage. It may even make you ineffective as a teacher if, for example, you teach health education or citizenship and it becomes public knowledge that you have a conviction for drug use or drunk and disorderly behaviour.

On the other hand, particularly if you are a young person, you need to balance your work and personal life. Your commitment to teaching should not be out of proportion to reasonable expectations of a "normal" life – with all that implies for the average person and their desire for a happy and fulfilled social and family life.

We all have different personal values. Discussing the scenarios above will have made clear what some of them are. We can look at them and take different standpoints – about the seriousness of the illegality of speeding or recreational drug use; about the morality of viewing adult pornography; about the inappropriateness of flirting or membership of extreme political parties. Don't think of them as a list of things that teachers must not do – they are not. But they are a thought-provoking exercise for how you need to manage the process of integrating your own set of personal values with a set of professional standards and practices as you enter a values-led profession such as teaching.

As discussed earlier, there is no difficulty in recruiting teachers any more. People are queuing up in droves. The problem these days is how to retain them. In the last two decades, an average of 25%–30% of teachers have left the profession within five years of entering it. Some of those are temporarily leaving to start families and may return later, but many leave because they find the responsibilities and accountabilities of teaching too onerous. For some, the whole experience feels overwhelming, especially where they cannot find a way to let off steam and balance their personal and social lives with work.

Balancing your work and social life, let alone your personal and professional personas, will be a major challenge for you in the early years of teaching. But you need to think about it now as one of the key issues in deciding whether teaching really is for you.

Reflections from the newteachersblogger – newteachersblog.wordpress.com

Taking the scenic route into teaching

Twenty years ago, I trained teachers at a London university. In those days it pioneered so-called Access courses to degree-level learning that are common now. The university positively targeted people who had no formal educational qualifications but who had one thing above all – a burning desire to learn.

It was obvious, even at interview stage, that some of these people were going to make wonderful teachers. They had bags of relevant experience, often through bringing up their own children; they had imagination, creativity, personal skills and passion. Then when they started the teacher-training course, they had commitment, stamina and resilience.

Some of the best people I ever trained as teachers started without a single GSCE to their name, let alone A levels. Many of them went on to be brilliant teachers, and now I come across some of them as successful and accomplished head teachers. My experience with those people not only continually inspired me but reminded me again and again of the wonderfully transformative power that teaching and education has – not just on the individuals involved and their families, but on society as a whole.

Case study

Janine's story

After being deterred from her initial interest in teaching by her bad experience on a work placement, Janine was inspired by her daughter first to volunteer at school, then work in a variety of teaching support roles, and eventually to qualify as a teacher herself.

"I never had a burning desire to be a teacher. In fact, when I was 15 I undertook two weeks of work experience in the nursery unit of a local primary school and wrote in my diary: "Having had this experience I know I will never work with children." It's funny how things change.

"I left school aged 16, with minimal GCSEs, to work in an office. I had my daughter when I was aged 18 and became a single parent on benefits. I did not want to be on benefits forever, though, so I spent the time between her birth and starting school attending college part-time to improve my GCSEs. I still had no desire to be a teacher at this point, I just wanted to get a job – any job – and come off benefits.

"When my daughter started primary school, the school asked for parents to volunteer listening to children read. My mum encouraged me to volunteer, saying it would get me out of the house and give me experience that would look good on a CV. So I began volunteering one morning a week – although this soon increased to a couple of mornings. Soon, I was asked by other teachers to help with their classes, and I ended up spending each afternoon as well as most mornings volunteering.

"Then, near the end of one term, I was told of a job at the school. It involved working at lunchtimes with some of the more difficult children by providing them with activities. This meant I was able to carry on volunteering as well. I got the job and at the same time began a part-time course at college – a City & Guilds in Learning Support. I thought that by doing this course I might be able to get a job in the future at the school as a teaching assistant, and that by having a qualification I would stand out above others.

"I wanted to become a teaching assistant as I really enjoyed working with the children, and being a single parent who didn't drive meant that I would have all the holidays off to be with my daughter. School hours also meant I could take her to and from school. Luckily, I got a job at my daughter's school and worked there in various roles ranging from lunchtime supervisor, classroom assistant, learning support assistant to cover supervisor and then unqualified teacher.

"After a few years, I did a Teaching Assistant NVQ level 3. I still had no ambition to be a teacher. I didn't think I would ever go to university. I thought I was quite happy to be a teaching assistant (TA) and just wanted to be the best I could be, and decided to continue to study. I then looked into becoming a Higher Level TA and went to the University of Northampton to listen to a talk about it. The talk also included information about the two-year Foundation Degree in Learning and Teaching. I was still under the impression that a TA is all I would ever be" – as one of the head teachers I had worked for told me.

"The thought of me – a single mum – going to university amazed me. I knew it would be hard work, but the thought of showing my daughter that there is a better life out there spurred me on. I took the Foundation degree and followed it up with a 12-month course to complete the BA (Hons) in Learning and Teaching (BALT). At the same time, I had to study for my maths and science GCSEs, as I needed them to proceed with the courses, and I felt that having the maths would help me in the future, whatever job I had. It was around this time that I became a cover supervisor, mainly covering classes when the class teacher was preparing and planning.

"I loved the freedom of teaching and the experience of it, but mostly I just enjoyed seeing the children learn and progress, knowing that I had a hand in it. Following the completion of the BALT course, I decided to wait until after my daughter did her own GCSEs before I pursued the next step, because if I went on to take another stressful qualification at the same time, we might kill each other!

"After my daughter finished her GCSEs, I decided to do the Graduate Teacher Programme (now known as School Direct), as I wanted to be able to continue to support and inspire her. I waited until last year before applying. Following what was to me a gruelling interview process, I got a much-coveted place on the course. This leads me back to where I am as I write – about to start my final term on the course.

"Now, finally, I know I can be a teacher. Deep down, I think I probably always did, but in the beginning when I left school I just didn't consider it to be a possibility. I guess what ultimately motivated me – apart from my love of teaching and learning – was my daughter, and the need to inspire and provide her with a better life."

2

The UK education system

The UK education system is the one of the most highly regarded in the world. It can encompass everything from provision for babies as young as three months in local day nurseries through to post-doctoral research at world-class universities.

However, this chapter concentrates on the school system rather than the whole of education in the UK – largely because if you are thinking of becoming a teacher, you will be trained specifically to teach in a school rather than a college or university.

The school system in the UK is not homogenous, neither does it share a common historical development. The system in England and Wales was only established with provision from the state in 1870, when the first elementary schools were set up. Until then, there were only private – still known widely as public – schools, or charitable education institutions established and supported by the Church of England. Scotland, however, has a longer and more varied history of free schooling. By 1902 local councils in Scotland were charged with creating "secondary schools", and extending education for children up to the age of 14.

The school system in the UK can be a little confusing, not least because it is divided into phases related to age ranges and into the constituent nations of England, Wales, Scotland and Northern Ireland, each with its own variation of school and examination system, the responsibility for which is devolved to the respective national government and departments. A whole book could be written on the variations across the UK, but while each system is distinct, there is also a good deal of similarity about them. For example, in every part of the UK there are very similar understandings of primary and secondary education, even if there are regional variations in jargon. Similarly, the precise detail of the school calendar varies around the country, generally running from September to July in most parts of England, in comparison to other parts of the UK. In Scotland, for example, it starts in August and runs through to late June.

In most parts of the UK, the system is divided into the same phases of early years, primary and secondary, but there are still some parts where a modified system – such as first, middle and secondary – still survives. These variations are not important for this book, and you will soon become familiar with them if you live in or move to such an area.

So don't worry, none of this is necessary to know in detail before going for interview with a training provider, and they certainly won't ask you questions about it. But it may help to read this chapter just to get acquainted with the structure of the system, especially if you are thinking of moving to an area of the UK where you may be unfamiliar with it.

The UK still has a tradition of faith schools, most of which were originally set up by the Church of England more than 150 years ago, although the concept has now expanded and diversified to include all the major faith groups. Faith schools comprise a large proportion of all schools in the UK; indeed, in some areas they predominate, so they are an important part of the picture.

Traditionally, the vast majority of schools in the UK have come under the umbrella of the maintained sector – better known as the state sector. These are schools funded and overseen by a local authority such as a city or county council. If you do decide to become a teacher anywhere in the UK, it is most likely that you will be employed by a school in the state sector, and the terms and conditions of your employment will probably be within the nationally agreed school teachers' pay and conditions document. As such, the main focus of this book will be centred on the structure and content of the state sector system, but there are other options available.

Nowadays, a growing proportion of schools are withdrawing from local authority control and adopting "academy" status, which means they effectively control themselves without reference to local authority accountability. Others, known as "free schools", are being set up with direct funding arrangements from central government, and have even greater freedom to determine their curriculum, syllabus and school ethos. Special schools are another important part of the mix. These are schools that provide education to children with special needs, such as behavioural, emotional, learning or social difficulties, or specific physical disabilities, such as hearing or visual impairment. Once again, most are governed and administered by local authorities. It is rare for teachers to train and to get their first job in a special school – the vast majority of teachers in such schools have first come through the mainstream system and then specialised at a later stage, although training courses are increasing their provision for students and trainees who are identifying at an early stage that special education is their preference.

Independent schools – or private schools as they are more commonly known – are entirely autonomous and operate as independent, not-for-profit businesses, although they are almost always registered as charities and organised within national umbrella independent-school associations of their own choosing. They often attract teachers without formal Qualified Teacher Status, but who are often highly qualified in specialist subject areas such as music, sciences or sports.

Profile: Bangor University & Aberystwyth University

The North and Mid-Wales Centre of Teacher Education

The North and Mid-Wales Centre of Teacher Education is a Centre of Excellence in Initial Teacher Education and Training. The Centre is a partnership between Aberystwyth and Bangor Universities. It offers a unique and vibrant experience for those wishing to pursue a career in teaching. The Centre provides the best possible start for trainee teachers in primary and secondary teaching.

What does this mean for you?

It means the best start possible for teacher training. The Centre of Teacher Education with the combined record of Bangor and Aberystwyth Universities, brings you quite simply more resources, more teachers, more partnership schools. In short, more support. It means that you have an unparalleled safety net of tutors and mentors, so that, as you embark on this most important and yet most challenging of careers, you do so knowing that as you stand in front of your class, you are on your own, but never alone.

Joint heritage

Both institutions delivering the teacher education courses at the Centre are well established and are among the oldest teacher training providers in the country, with an exceptional tradition of quality and success in the training and education of teachers.

Centre partners are both located in county's considered to be the some of the safest in the UK, offering peace of mind to students.

Partnership schools

The Centre works with more than 500 partnership schools across North and Mid-Wales. Both campuses have well-established partnerships with Primary and Secondary Schools to provide varied and supportive training environments for students. The Centre has designated University trained Senior and Subject mentors in schools supported by University link tutors, as well as a comprehensive pastoral support structure for trainees while on School experience.

Centre location

The Centre is located on 2 main campuses across Aberystwyth University and Bangor University. Both campuses are relatively compact in nature, making it easy for students to get around. Centre partners enjoy being situated in unspoilt, welcoming university towns situated by the sea and mountains.

Training salaries of up to £20,000 are available for some subjects, depending on your degree classification.

For more information (Bangor), please visit
www.bangor.ac.uk/education

For more information (Aberystwyth), please visit
www.aber.ac.uk/sell

The maintained (or state) sector

Schools in the state system in England and Wales are required to follow the National Curriculum, which is made up of 12 subjects.

There are three core subjects that are compulsory for all children aged 5 to 16, and these are:

1. English

2. mathematics

3. science.

Then there are foundation subjects. These are also compulsory, but only at one or more of some of the Key Stages. Then there are other subjects that are non-statutory within the National Curriculum, such as religious education at all Key Stages, sex education from Key Stage 2 onwards, and careers education in Key Stages 3 and 4. Religious education may be withdrawn for individual pupils by parental request, and parents may also choose to remove their child from some or all sex education lessons.

The vast majority of schools in the UK are within the state sector, and, in England particularly, they are organised within a bewildering array of governance arrangements for how they recruit staff and admit pupils; who owns and manages buildings; and the extent to which they are free to set their own syllabus and curriculum.

- **Community schools.** These used to be known as "county schools". In community schools, the local authority employs all the staff, owns the buildings and property and has complete responsibility for the admission of the pupils. The governors of the school come from a variety of community backgrounds, including nominations by political parties represented on the local council, and from parents and teachers.

- **Voluntary controlled schools.** These are faith schools, usually associated with the Church of England. The property and buildings are commonly owned by a charitable foundation, although in most cases the local authority employs the staff and is responsible for the admission of pupils.

- **Voluntary aided schools.** Again, these are usually faith schools, most often affiliated to the Church of England or the Roman Catholic Church, although sometimes they are non-denominational schools affiliated to "Livery Companies" or parochial and charitable trusts. If so, the charitable foundation contributes towards the capital costs of the school, such as the property and buildings, and will have a significant role in appointing the school governors – roles that will often include members of the parish as well as community. In contrast, the governing body of the school will employ the staff and is responsible for admissions.

- **Foundation schools.** The school land and buildings are owned by the governing body or by a charitable foundation, and the foundation appoints many of the governors and in turn employs the staff and is responsible for admissions.

- **Academy schools.** These are a relatively new development, established by the Labour government (1997–2010) to replace poorly performing community schools in areas of high social and economic deprivation. Their start-up costs are typically funded privately, for example by entrepreneurs or social, non-governmental organisations, with running costs met by the Department for Education (DfE). They are exempt from direct local authority control and their numbers are expanding rapidly at the current coalition government's encouragement. Academies are mainly secondary schools, but in recent years have extended to the primary sector.

- **Free schools.** These were introduced as a new initiative in England by the coalition government. They allow parents, teachers, charities or businesses to set up a school where there is a perceived local need for more provision. They have been controversial in that they are funded by the taxpayer but not under local authority control. As with foundation schools and academies, they are accountable to the Secretary of State for Education, although they are not academically selective and are free to attend.

All state-funded schools are regularly inspected by the Office for Standards in Education (Ofsted) and publish reports on the quality of education at a particular school after an inspection. Schools judged by Ofsted to be providing an inadequate standard of education may be subject to special measures, which could include replacing the governing body and senior staff.

The school system in England and Wales

Schooling in England and Wales is compulsory from the age of 5 until 17 (and will rise to 18 in 2015). It is divided into four phases:

1. the early years: ages 3 to 4+

2. primary education: ages 4+ to 11

3. secondary education: ages 11 to 18

4. post-secondary education or tertiary education: 18+.

Nursery and early years

While full-time compulsory education does not begin until the age of 5, most children from the age of 3 will be able to access a place at a local authority-funded nursery or nursery school. Children are taught on the basis of the Early Years Foundation Stage curriculum. It sets out requirements for both welfare and for learning and development. These include targets that, by the age of 5, children should:

- readily use written language in their play and learning

- use phonic knowledge to write simple regular words and make phonetically plausible attempts at more complex words

- show an understanding of how information can be found in non-fiction texts to answer questions about where, who, why and how

- begin to form simple sentences, sometimes using punctuation.

There are similar requirements for numeracy that include providing children with opportunities to:

- develop and improve their skills in counting

- understand and use numbers

- calculate simple addition and subtraction problems

- describe, shapes, spaces and measures.

While many local authority nurseries are located independently from schools, some are physically attached as school nurseries, located alongside and often as an integral part of a primary school. Children will transfer from a nursery to the Reception class of an infant or primary school, usually during the term when they reach the age of 5.

Class sizes can range up to 26 children in nursery and Reception classes, but the current regulations require the adult-to-child ratio to be 1:13. However, you will typically find a lower ratio than that, with a number of additional nursery nurses or teaching assistants adding to the core teaching staff.

For more details about the Early Years Foundation Stage in England, please visit:

- www.education.gov.uk/schools/teachingandlearning/curriculum/a0068102/early-years-foundation-stage-eyfs

- http://foundationyears.org.uk

Wales introduced a new, Foundation phase of education that has now extended to 7-year-olds, and is often described as far more practical and experiential than its English counterpart. For example, teachers in Wales are given more freedom to encourage children to build their self-esteem and positive attitudes to learning through a greater emphasis on creativity and practical learning experiences. Welsh schools can also offer teaching in the medium of the Welsh language, and Welsh language teaching is compulsory at up to age 16. Currently, about 20%–25% of all schools in Wales teach in Welsh for most or all of the time.

Primary

Primary schooling is often divided between:

- infants schools: attended by children from 4+ to 7+

- junior schools: attended by children 7+ to 11+

– although they are also combined and known as infants and junior or primary schools.

Most children start school at the beginning of the academic year during which they are five years old (although compulsory schooling is required only from the term *after* their fifth birthday).

All children being taught in state-funded infants, junior and primary schools follow the National Curriculum through the:

- Foundation Stage curriculum in Reception class

- Key Stage 1 curriculum at Year 1 and Year 2

- Key Stage 2 curriculum at Year 3, Year 4, Year 5 and Year 6.

The National Curriculum subjects taught in primary schools (until 2014) are:

- English

- mathematics

- science

- physical education (PE)

- personal, social and health education (PSHE)

- information and communications technology (ICT), although there is freedom for schools to design their own programmes of study for this now

- history

- geography

- music

- design and technology (D&T)

- art and design;

and

there is non-statutory guidance to teach both religious education (RE) and modern foreign languages (MFL) at Key Stages 1 and 2.

There are proposals for a revised National Curriculum that, if implemented, will come into force in September 2014. For the purposes of considering teaching as a career, we need not enter into too much detail about these. They are relatively minor and, although important to those teaching them, will largely affect the emphasis given to the content of various programmes of study. So, for example, in ICT there will be much less emphasis on desktop publishing skills and much more on developing young people's ability to code and write computer programs; in geography there will be more emphasis on the study and effects of climate change; and for MFL there will be greater freedom in primary schools to choose which languages to study. However, by the time you complete a teacher-training course these proposals will have been further refined and, if implemented, embedded in practice.

Assessments at this stage are known as Key Stage 1 Standard Attainment Tests (SATs, formerly known as Standard Attainment Tasks) and take place in Year 2 (the end of infants) throughout May of each year. All children are assessed by their teacher in reading and writing (including spelling and handwriting); maths (number, shape, space and measurement); and science. This method of testing is known as Teacher Assessment, because it relies on the knowledge and judgement of the teacher rather than a standardised test. SATs are divided into levels of attainment, and children are expected to reach Level 2 in those subjects by the end of Key Stage 1.

More formal Key Stage 2 SATs take place in mid-May for all children in Year 6 and apply to the three core subjects:

- **English (including grammar and spelling)**

- **maths**

- **science.**

Children are expected to reach Level 4 – this is the level deemed average for a child of 11 – in these core subjects by the time they leave primary school, although able children may be assessed by teachers to see whether they can reach Level 5 or even Level 6. Key Stage 2 test papers are not marked by the child's teacher but are sent for independent marking and moderation, with results made available before the end of term. Controversially, they go on to determine the position of the school in the league tables published both locally and nationally. The government has announced plans to revise aspects of the assessment system for 2014–15, whereby all children will be given an individualised ranking at Key Stage 2 that will indicate to parents the attainment of their children in direct comparison to other children in their class and cohort.

Currently, there are also additional informal assessments taken by a child's teacher (like the teacher assessments at Key Stage 1) in history, geography and ICT, but these are not used for determining the position of the school in the league tables.

In Wales, as part of the new Foundation stage, the Welsh Government scrapped Key Stage 1 assessments completely, and all Welsh schools now do only teacher assessments at the end of Key Stage 2.

Profile: University of Southampton

UNIVERSITY OF
Southampton

Show your class and learn to teach at Southampton

At the University of Southampton, our wide range of education programmes can help set you on the road to an outstanding career in teaching.

You can choose from our extensive range of teacher-training options and benefit from our strong partnerships with more than 400 regional schools and colleges. As well as PGCE training in Primary, Secondary and Further Education, we also offer an innovative new training route – PGCE School Direct.

Adrian Halnan, Director of Programmes at Southampton Education School (SES), says: "Our partnerships with schools and colleges ensure our students gain practical experience to support their studies. These strong links allow us to provide a good balance between school-based and university-based study.

"At Southampton we don't have a one-size-fits-all approach but are committed to being flexible and providing a programme that meets the trainees' future career needs. We strive to ensure our trainees have the right balance of knowledge, practical experience and skills, so they can start a successful teaching career."

At SES, we are looking for trainees who aspire to be the next generation of outstanding teachers. Our research culture and high-quality programmes empower our students to think critically about teaching and learning. They are encouraged to take risks, solve problems, be self-critical and experimental.

Our experienced academics, who maintain strong links with policy-makers, are involved in the latest research. Our Director of Initial Teacher Education, Kate Green, is regularly invited to the Westminster Education Forum to share her insights into the future of teacher training with the key figures in the UK's education sector.

PGCE Secondary alumna Becky Jannaway said: "The training on this course has challenged me to be innovative and professional in my chosen career, and has succeeded in supporting me on my path to becoming an outstanding teacher. I can safely say that I have been trained by dedicated and motivated professionals, and would highly recommend anyone considering teaching as their career to begin their journey at the University of Southampton."

Many of our PGCE trainees also get the chance to be part of a trip to Africa to gain invaluable experience where the availability of different teaching resources forms a unique challenge, even for an experienced teacher.

PGCE Secondary alumnus Rob McGough said: "I had always intended to develop myself as a teacher in Kenya, and the chance to experience a curriculum in a different culture and cope with limited resources enhanced my skills. I feel as though I left the country with not just extra classroom skills but unforgettable memories, brilliant new friends and a little piece of my heart left on another continent."

Come and join our thriving education community here at SES – show your class, to become a successful teacher and begin a rewarding career in teaching.

To find out more about studying at SES, please visit www.southampton.ac.uk/showyourclass.

Class sizes in primary schools

Class sizes in infants schools (Reception through to Year 2) typically number around 25, although in many areas of the country there have been considerable pressures that have put that policy under strain, and teachers in infants schools and departments are regularly taking classes with more than 25 children in them.

Thirty children is typical for junior classes (Years 3 to 6) in primary schools, although many schools fund the employment of additional TAs to bring down the adult-to-child ratio and support the effectiveness of the class teacher.

Even as a new teacher, you would find yourself managing TAs either on a regular or occasional basis. While these are not qualified teachers, they are often well trained and very able, particularly if they have a specific responsibility for children with a special need. However, you will by and large find yourself solely responsible for a class of around 30 children, and there will be regular occasions when you will find yourself teaching with little or no additional support; this is the norm in some schools.

For more on the primary curriculum in England, please visit:

www.gov.uk/national-curriculum/key-stage–1–2

Secondary

In most areas of England and Wales, children will transfer from a primary school to a secondary school at age 11; although there are still one or two places where first, middle and upper or high-school arrangements are in place, where transfer ages are slightly different, but these are disappearing.

As with primary schooling, secondary education in England and Wales comprises the National Curriculum, and all its Core and Foundation subjects are taught. In Wales the teaching of the Welsh language is also compulsory up to the age of 16.

The National Curriculum subjects taught in secondary schools (until 2014), at both Key Stages 3 and 4, are:

- English

- mathematics

- science

- PE

- PSHEE

- citizenship

- ICT (although schools are now free to design their own programmes of study for this)

and at Key Stage 3 only:

- history

- geography

- music

- D&T

- art & design

- MFL.

For RE, there is non-statutory guidance to teach the subject at both Key Stages 3 and 4.

For more on the secondary school curriculum in England, please visit: www.gov.uk/national-curriculum/key-stage–3–4

Table 1. Summary of the structure of schooling in England and Wales

Child's Age	England & Wales school years	SATs	Curriculum stage		Schools
3–4	Nursery		Foundation Stage (Wales: to the end of Year 2)	Nursery and early years	
5	Reception			Infants	Primary
6	1		Key Stage 1		
7	2	KS1			
8	3		Key Stage 2	Junior	
9	4				
10	5				
11	6	KS2			
12	7		Key Stage 3	Secondary	Secondary with sixth form
13	8				
14	9	KS3			
15	10		Key Stage 4		
16	11	KS4 GCSEs			
17	12	AS levels	Key Stage 5	Sixth-form or Further Education college	
18	13	KS5 A levels			

The school system in Scotland

Scotland has a quite distinct education system from the rest of the UK, but, although it does not follow the National Curriculum of England and Wales, there are similarities in both structure and content. It is called the 5–14 Programme, and perhaps the biggest contrast with the rest of the UK is the greater flexibility of this system. For example, parents can opt for their children to have an additional year at nursery (depending on their date of birth), primary pupils remain at school for seven rather than six years, transferring at 12 rather than 11 years old, and the secondary curriculum and exam system allows for much greater breadth, so that students go to university with a much wider knowledge of subjects compared to the very narrow focus of their counterparts in England, Wales and Northern Ireland.

Education at all levels is the responsibility of the Scottish Parliament and the Scottish Government's Education and Lifelong Learning Department – Education Scotland – and state-maintained schools are all owned and managed by the 32 local education authorities. Whereas in England, inspections of school standards are conducted by Ofsted (and in Wales by Estyn), Scotland has three bodies: the Care Inspectorate for pre-school provision; Her Majesty's Inspectorate of Education for primary and secondary education, and the Quality Assurance Agency for Higher Education (QAA Scotland). Scotland's inspectors also tend to have less notoriety in the eyes of many English and Welsh teachers. Qualifications at secondary schools in Scotland are provided by the Scottish Qualifications Authority, and almost all children will take the Scottish Qualifications Certificate at the Standard National Grade and later the Highers and Advanced Highers in preparation for university entry.

The school system in Northern Ireland

Education policy in Northern Ireland is determined by the Department for Education in Northern Ireland (www.deni.gov.uk), while responsibility for and administration of schooling is delegated to five local Education and Library Boards. The school year in Northern Ireland runs from the beginning of September to the end of June, and although the structure and content of the system is similar in most respects to other parts of the UK, its character is of course distinctive in that it reflects Northern Ireland's divided society. Some schools in Northern Ireland are integrated but most are not, and the type and naming of schools is usually a reflection of their religious denomination. Even controlled schools, which are non-denominational, are attended mainly by members of the Protestant community, whereas voluntary maintained schools are mainly Roman Catholic.

The exam system in Northern Ireland is closer to the English GCSE and A level system than it is to the Scottish exam system, but its performance is remarkable in that it regularly outperforms the other UK nations.

Table 2. Summary of the structure of schooling in Scotland and Northern Ireland

Age at the start of the school year	Age at the end of the school year	School years in Scotland	School years in Northern Ireland
3–4	4–5	Nursery	Primary year 1 – Key Stage 1
4–5	5–6	Primary 1	Primary year 2
5–6	6–7	Primary 2	Primary year 3
6–7	7–8	Primary 3	Primary year 4 – Key Stage 2
7–8	8–9	Primary 4	Primary year 5
8–9	9–10	Primary 5	Primary year 6
9–10	10–11	Primary 6	Primary year 7
10–11	11–12	Primary 7	Secondary year 8 – Key Stage 3
11–12	12–13	Secondary S1 (first year)	Secondary year 9
12–13	13–14	Secondary S2 (second year)	Secondary year 10
13–14	14–15	Secondary S3 (third year) National 3 and 4	Secondary year 11 – Key Stage 4
14–15	15–16	Secondary S4 (fourth year) National 4 or 5	Secondary year 12 GCSEs
15–16	16–17	Secondary S5 (fifth year) National 5 or Higher	Secondary year 13
16–17	17–18	Secondary S6 (sixth year) Higher or Advanced Higher	Secondary year 14 A levels

Teachers' conditions, pay and pensions in the UK

Once again, there are minor variations across the UK, and details of these can be found at relevant government websites or teacher union websites (see 'Further resources and information', p.239). However, the general picture for those considering teaching as a career at entry level is remarkably uniform across the country. You would recognise the conditions, pay and pensions of teachers from one end of the country to another – apart from London, which has pay scales specific to the costs of accommodation and travel. The arrangements are as follows.

- Teachers must be available for work 195 days a year (this includes five days that will be spent on training and development: In-Service Education and Training (INSET) days).

- Within the 195 days, there are 1,265 hours known as directed time where teachers can be assigned various duties by school management, usually the head teacher.

- Teachers are also required to work extra hours (not specified) to ensure that they fulfil their professional duties – such as planning, preparing, marking, carrying out assessments and writing reports.

- However, teachers are entitled to 10% PPA time – for planning, preparation and assessment – as part of their weekly timetable.

- Teachers do not have to supervise children having lunch at lunchtimes, do not have to carry out routine administrative duties that can be delegated to support staff, and should not have to cover the absence of colleagues for more than 38 hours a year.

There is a unified pay scale for nursery, primary and secondary teachers in England and Wales, but the management responsibilities in larger schools – both primary and secondary – allow for greater opportunity to earn higher salaries. As a general indication (based on 2013 information) a new teacher can expect a starting salary of:

- around £22,000 outside the so-called "inner London" boroughs

- around £27,000 in inner London.

Remaining on the main scale, without any responsibilities, this can rise to a maximum of £32,000 and £37,000 respectively. An experienced teacher, perhaps running a department and having achieved relevant and appropriate standards, could expect up to £57,000 a year outside London. Head teachers in the primary sector are earning anywhere between £37,000 for a small rural school and £80,000+ depending on the size of the institution and the nature of additional responsibilities. Some secondary head teachers are earning above £100,000, especially in London.

For details of teachers' pay scales, please visit:

www.education.gov.uk/get-into-teaching/salary/pay-and-benefits

or at a number of teaching union sites, including:

www.teachers.org.uk/payandconditions/pay

The ranges for Scotland (which can be found at www.eis.org.uk/Pay_and_ Conditions_of_Service/salary_scales.htm) and Northern Ireland are similar, minus the additions for London of course.

In spite of recent government changes to teachers' pension benefits, and the ongoing controversy over these for teaching unions, teachers' pensions are based on a career average salary, and remain one of the most attractive and secure in the public sector. In spite of the changes, they remain for the foreseeable future a positive asset in the benefit portfolio for teachers.

3

Choosing who and what to teach

If you think you'd like to be a teacher because young children are really cute, love to learn and will respond enthusiastically to every idea you put to them, think again.

If you think you'd like to teach teenagers because they're more mature, sophisticated and you can reason with them, forget that too.

In fact, forget all the preconceptions you have about children of any age, because you'll find them all confounded by the time you've completed your first week in the classroom.

On the other hand, it goes without saying that you are basing your decision of which phase and specialism you want to teach on some perception of what children are like, and an assessment of the skills and knowledge you have to offer. Just don't be naïve about it, or you might find yourself getting disillusioned rather quickly.

Getting school experience before you start

These days it is almost impossible to get on a teacher-training course of whatever kind without having had some experience of working or volunteering with children and young people, especially in a school setting.

All training providers are looking for people who know why they want to be teachers. Having some experience of working with children – even if that's only volunteering with readers in your local primary school – will help them assess you.

Better than that, it will help you too . . .

- First, you'll be able to see what the job is about – getting school experience will give you a real insight into the workings of teaching. You'll be able to see it close up, warts and all.

- You'll be able to meet teachers, and ask them some searching questions about the rewards they get and the sacrifices they make. They won't need any encouragement to tell you the unvarnished truth!

- You'll be able to meet children – volunteering in a school for a few weeks might make up your mind that you love them, you hate them or you just don't get them. It might also help you decide that, while teaching is definitely for you, teenagers or secondary schools are not your thing . . . or the other way round.

- It'll help you prepare for your training interview – without school experience (or any kind of volunteering experience with children), it will be hard to reflect on the issues the training provider will raise with you.

However, getting school experience can present a few practical problems, especially if you are in full-time employment and really can't take time off to volunteer. There are also hurdles such as criminal record checks and so on. Schools have become very conscious of security issues and safeguarding children in recent years.

Nevertheless, you will have to overcome these practical problems. If it means having to take some annual holiday time to volunteer, or use your evenings to get involved with Scouts, Guides or other voluntary organisations for young people, or pay the £30+ yourself to have a criminal record check done just to get the privilege of volunteering in a school for a few weeks, then this is something you may just have to accept if you really want to be a teacher.

But how do I go about it?

- Ask the head teacher of a local school – offer personal references if necessary.

- Ask the head teacher of a school you once attended.

- If you really can't find time to volunteer at a school during the day because of work, ask the head teacher whether there are any after-school clubs you can get involved with, or ask the leader of local Scouts, Guides, Cadets or Youth Club.

More information about gaining school experience can be found at www.education.gov.uk.

The way you plan and prepare, the teaching strategies you use, the curriculum and the syllabus on offer will be determined to a large extent by the phase and subjects you are teaching. So, while teaching a nursery class of four-year-olds may be a different world to teaching an A-level physics group of 17-year-olds, it also has its similarities. The nature of teaching is essentially one of leading, and that is true whomsoever you teach. The differences are in the stages of intellectual development and the content and subject matter.

Let's take a look at the various phases on offer, and try to describe the characteristics of the children you'll find there and the nature of the tasks that are specific to the school context at various phases.

Nursery and early years

Nursery education is not the same as child-minding. It is not about letting young children wander in a softly furnished environment freely choosing to paint, play in the sand pit or career round a play area on three-wheeled bicycles while the teachers, nursery nurses and assistants wipe snotty noses here and there. It has a theory and a rigour every bit as demanding and complex as any other area of education. Indeed, because it involves dealing with a stage of life that is so dynamic and fast developing, it is arguably much more demanding and interesting than teaching older children.

The Early Years Foundation Stage is the government's framework of standards for all teachers and providers working in the early years and nursery sector. It sets out 17 early-learning goals, but emphasises three areas that are considered most essential for a child's healthy development. These are:

- **communication and language**

- **physical**

- **personal, social and emotional development.**

However, the needs of very young children clearly differ from older ones in that some of their basic needs, such as eating, drinking, dressing and going to the toilet may require some physical assistance or regulation in ways that those of older children do not. If you are not familiar with a nursery school environment – or have forgotten what it was like – you will see that nursery teachers arrange a nursery as a learning environment rather than a teaching environment. They are primarily organising the nursery so that young children can discover and explore the world around them.

Nursery teachers and their colleagues will be found busily arranging a variety of learning environments – zones if you like – with which children can engage. Their interventions will be most often to persuade, encourage and usher children from one to the other, rather than formally timetable them. When they are to be found teaching, they will be sitting alongside young children asking them questions and assisting them to enquire and explore, not instructing or directing them. Of course, there will be occasions when children will be helped to learn skills such as holding knives, forks and spoons or fastening buttons or tying shoelaces, possibly acquiring such skills for the first time in their lives. Nursery teachers will also be creating authentic opportunities for children to learn to hold and manipulate pencils, pens, paintbrushes and other tools for expressive and educational ends – but the emphasis in a nursery is always on the heuristic aspects of learning and discovery.

So the role of a nursery teacher, while primarily educative, has pastoral, social and emotional responsibilities interwoven to a greater extent than for teachers of older children. Nursery teachers must be highly sensitive to all kinds of basic needs for young children because these children will be more reliant on the teacher to provide for them. Older children, who have more developed linguistic and social skills, can access wider social networks, such as their friends and peers.

Young children will, by and large, have relatively limited language development and will be less able to articulate at the age of four or five, so their needs – both educational and social – may need sensitive interpretation. As an adjunct to this, nursery teachers also need to be extremely acute at observing young children. Indeed, part of their daily tasks will be to record how children are responding to opportunities to explore and discover, and to challenges such as whether they can hold a knife and fork or a paintbrush unaided, identify colours, recognise their name label on a tray or coat-hanger or order objects according to weight or size. As a nursery teacher you will, almost like a proud parent, be watching carefully for such developments – especially if they have been a long time coming.

Nurseries, like all schooling environments, are highly governed by routine and the rhythm of the day, even though the teacher has made it look free and relaxed. Some activities, such as story-time, will be done as a group to develop a sense of community and awareness of others. At such times, the teacher may be mediating the children's varying responses to the story, skilfully finding ways of including comments to contrive a common appreciation of the story.

Other activities, such as playing in water trays or sand pits, will be relatively unsupervised so a child can explore at his or her own pace of curiosity. While it may seem like aimless play, the way such activities are constructed by the teacher will lead children to explore fundamental scientific or mathematical concepts such as conservation or compression – for instance, whether a long thin vessel holding water has the same capacity as a short wide one, or whether some solids, such as sand, can behave like liquids or whether air can be compressed in a balloon or contained in a bubble. Through play activities they will discover the properties of liquids, solids and gases. This is not just play, this is the beginning of mathematical conceptualisation and scientific inquiry, and nursery teachers must have a detailed understanding of what is going on. But it is also play in that children will learn to take turns, make up procedures, operate within constraints and choose teams or partners – in other words, they learn that it is behaviour governed by the same rules they will later learn from taking part in society. While the activities of a nursery may have the appearance of being unstructured or chaotic, they are anything but.

Other early learning activities you will see may involve the beginnings of what the lay person might recognise as teaching – where nursery staff may be found working alongside children who are matching, threading, counting or ordering. Whatever the activities, working in a nursery is perhaps the most physically demanding of all teaching jobs. You will certainly know you have done a day's work after being in a nursery – there will be a lot of bending, crouching, twisting, turning, lifting and moving about.

Perhaps the most striking thing you will notice about a nursery school environment is how apparently independent and autonomous the children seem in deciding what activities they choose – but this is largely down to the skill of a nursery teacher. They organise and structure the environment of the nursery so that children's curiosity can be aroused and stimulated by a range of physical, tactile, audio-sensory and social activities throughout their day with the minimum of regimentation.

The physical structure of a nursery is a fascinating array of zones or areas designed to engage children in different aspects of their early education, both inside and outside the building – standard resources will include equipment such as climbing frames, tunnels and play apparatus. Others areas will contain water, sand or building blocks. Inside, there will be areas for quiet reflection, such as book corners, or where children can explore personal relationships – areas with dressing-up boxes, where children can role-play being shopkeepers, doctors, nurses, firefighters or policemen, and so on.

But as a nursery teacher, your organisational skills will be a premium, because however pliable and amiable young children can appear, they will soon become distracted and disorderly without the expert management required to guide, direct and engage them implicitly.

Patience is a quality all teachers need, but perhaps it is most valuable in a nursery teacher because young children are at the earliest stages of manipulative skill and intellectual and emotional development, so they need more time to acquire even a basic grasp and understanding of new concepts. A young and sensitive child will keenly feel even the least hint of frustration or impatience demonstrated by a teacher. They may not yet have the intellectual development to reflect on their limited understanding, or the linguistic skill to express it in the way older children will be able to.

Young children in a nursery may not be able to say "I don't understand" or "I don't know" – they will more often just look bemused. A nursery teacher must not only be trained to respond to those signs, but have a patient and encouraging personality to respond to them.

As a nursery teacher, you will work closely with parents. It is not untypical that parents, usually mothers, will spend a few hours of the first few days, if not the first week or two, helping their child settle into their new environment. After that, almost daily consultation with parents about how their child is progressing is the norm, with everything from what they have eaten that day to how well they painted a picture or played with friends.

Another thing you'll notice about nursery and early years teachers is that they are almost always women. Such a demographic may have been self-evident to you, but if working with both men and women is important to you, then a nursery school probably won't be the environment for you.

People who go into nursery and early years teaching will be those who are fascinated by child development. The early stages of young children's physical and intellectual development and language acquisition can be the most absorbing topics in education, and are often the most written and theorised about. So don't think that this area of schooling will make any less of an intellectual demand on you – it won't.

Nursery teachers are also people who like the physical, tactile and intimate side of teaching young children. If you choose this career, you will be working closely with young children, observing, nurturing, enabling and coaching them in the earliest and most basic of concepts and skills, knowledge and behaviours. And yes . . . you will have to regularly wipe some snotty noses (or worse!), dab a few tears from the cheeks of a child who is missing their mummy, and give comforting cuddles to children who have fallen off their bicycle or the climbing frame. Nursery teaching, in all its complexity, is the clearest example in the teaching profession of its theory, craft and duty of care being demonstrably combined.

Profile: University of Chester

Chester: A unique blend of tradition and innovation

If you want to join a growing family of committed and outstanding teachers, there are a variety of pathways that you can choose at Chester.

For serving teachers, there are the postgraduate certificates, master's and EdD programmes, as well as short subject-knowledge-enhancement programmes, many of which take place on regular "master's weekends" at the university's Riverside Campus. School leavers choose either the BA Primary Education with Qualified Teacher Status or a degree such as our Early Childhood Studies programme followed by a Postgraduate Certificate of Education (PGCE) to enter the teaching profession.

The university benefits from deep and enduring partnerships with schools in the region, many of which are led and staffed by alumni. The faculty has pioneered many initiatives over the years and is currently the Higher Education Institution partner of choice for more than 20 school alliances working on the new School Direct Teacher Education programmes.

The teaching-led, research-informed Faculty of Education and Children's Services also provides a range of courses for the wider children's workforce. The Faculty has a rising research profile, including a research centre focused on Research in Education and the Arts through Practice (RECAP) and a research unit for transprofessionalism in public services.

The faculty has many established international partnerships and a mature internationalisation strategy affording opportunities for students and staff to work with others in the field of education around the world.

In choosing to study at Chester, you are making a link to a long-established history. It was in 1839 when William Gladstone, the Earl of Derby and John Sumner, Bishop of Chester and subsequently Archbishop of Canterbury, founded a teacher training college in the city. The original buildings in the ancient city of Chester, now Senate House of the University of Chester, were the first in the country to be purpose-built for the professional training of teachers.

In the intervening 175 years, the institution has grown into a modern, multi-faculty university, still committed to innovation in education. It continues to provide high-quality education and development for teachers in purpose-designed curriculum spaces in the impressive Faculty building – Riverside, which was once Cheshire's County Hall on the banks of the River Dee within the ancient walls of the City of Chester. This makes it a unique blend of tradition and innovation.

Primary

Schools are communities, and often reflect the community of their immediate neighbourhood. This is especially true for most primary schools in the UK where the catchment – the area the pupil intake is drawn from – is the immediate residential proximity. Most parents are happy to send their children to the local primary school and so they tend to reflect, much more than with even nursery and secondary schools, the demographic profile of the neighbourhood. For many teachers, that is the great appeal of teaching in a primary school – you get to serve the local community – and if you have grown up in that community, you may be a particularly valuable asset to them.

If the idea of building up a long-term and in-depth knowledge of the development of a relatively small group of children appeals to you, then working in a primary school will suit you to a tee. Unlike secondary schools, you will have the opportunity to spend most if not all of the day with the same group of children. You will get to know, intimately, their strengths and weaknesses, their personality and character, their moods and humours.

You will get to know their parents too, particularly their mothers, because in primary schools children are, by and large, still brought to and picked up from school every day, so you will regularly interact with parents and family members. This adds a dimension to the teaching that, for the most part, will be enormously valuable, as parents can regularly provide you with an insight into aspects of their child's ability, aptitude and behaviour that might be completely hidden to you.

Primary school teachers have also been very innovative in recent decades in involving parents in their children's education – it is now common for primary schools to have family literacy and numeracy schemes.

Like nursery schools, primary school staff are made up largely of women. Nationally, the average proportion of women in primary teaching is around 85%, and in some schools this will be even higher.

However, the major noticeable characteristic about primary teachers is that there is a degree of flexibility in comparison to more subject-oriented secondary colleagues. While primary schools in recent years have concentrated much more on the core areas of literacy and numeracy (and successive governments have promoted national strategies in these subject areas since the mid-1990s), they still have a considerable degree of freedom to be creative where they have the encouragement and the initiative to use it.

While teaching broadly within the subject-oriented National Curriculum, primary teachers have a good deal of latitude in how Curriculum subjects are delivered. This is largely because of what we know about how young children learn. They do not see the world divided into subject areas; it is not (yet) categorised into a mathematical world, a scientific world, a historical world or a geographical world and so on. For them, the world is still an amorphous mass of integrated and undifferentiated physical and emotional experience that they need the help of a teacher to make increasing categorical sense of. Compartmentalising the world into subjects can be highly counterproductive for a young child – not least because they don't necessarily understand why you would want or need to turn the experience of eating a pizza into a maths lesson on fractions!

Good primary school teachers, though, try to arouse the natural curiosity and interest that children bring to school with them, and then structure it with formal methods such as linguistic, mathematical and scientific concepts to extend understanding and build intellectual capacity.

For example, children can be enormously aroused and interested by mini-beasts, such as spiders, snails and worms, which they may find in their back gardens or even in the grounds of the school or a local park. Primary school teachers may use the heading of 'mini-beasts' as a topic or project within which to teach, study and apply a range of National Curriculum subjects. So, you might see a creative primary teacher using spiders to explore questions such as the following.

- **What is a spider? How are they different from insects? (counting legs, observing thorax, species identification, biology – mathematics and science)**

- **How do spiders differ? Are garden spiders the same as house spiders? (how they make different webs – identification – science; classification – mathematics)**

- Why do spiders build webs? (the pattern and structure of a web, spirals – mathematics, D&T)

- How do spiders create their thread? (what it is made of, what its properties are – biology, chemistry, general science)

- What is the structure and strength of those webs? (testing the strength of similar structures – forces, physics, general science, mathematics, D&T)

- How do spiders differ from country to country? (in size, colouring, habitat – geography)

A good primary teacher will then supplement such questions with practical activities that will allow the children to closely observe, describe, read about, research (ICT), write about, record (English, literacy), draw, paint, photograph, video (ICT, art and design) and experiment (science) – which will inevitably employ, practise and develop various other skills such as reading, writing, speaking. They will also enhance the overall experience by doing things like reading aloud stories of literary merit, such as the classic *Charlotte's Web*, or exploring related music, poetry and dance, such as the tarantella.

In short, primary schools still retain a good deal of opportunity for teachers to be creative and innovative. especially where a self-confident and visionary head teacher encourages and instils confidence in their staff to take risks and not be completely hide-bound by the drive to meet subject-based SAT targets.

The reality, of course, is that most schools are very focused on ensuring the core key skills of literacy and numeracy are taught efficiently and effectively, to reach the standards on which the school will be primarily judged – not just by parents, but crucially by Ofsted when they come to inspect. So don't be surprised if some of that idealistic creativity that might have inspired you to become a primary teacher has to be tempered somewhat by the realities of an educational system that is dominated by political imperatives. Politicians like to say that they "leave teaching to the teachers", but the target-driven, league-table-dominated system that they create and maintain largely determines how schools and teachers must respond.

Most primary class sizes are around 30 children. They will most often be sitting in chairs at tables (rather than desks) because the teacher will sometimes want to organise the children to learn in groups around "island" tables.

Most primary schools in the UK, however, are small — and almost always smaller than secondary schools — averaging around 250–350 pupils per school. Village primary schools in rural areas may even consist of a couple of mixed-age classes of around 50–60 pupils in total, while in some inner-city areas you will find large confederated primary schools of 1,000 or more pupils.

Even in large primary schools, though, the ethos is very much one of being a small community where the head teacher will, or will at least try to, know every child's name, where the children are likely to know each other and each other's families and where there is a general atmosphere of mutual caring, intimacy and friendship.

People who want to become primary school teachers are usually those who are more interested in the way children learn and develop rather than the subjects and content of the curriculum they are taught. While many secondary teachers will freely admit they have a passion for their subject, most primary teachers get their joy from seeing children learn to read a book for the first time, master their multiplication tables and solve mathematical problems, observe natural phenomena, such as a spider spinning a web, or make a scientific discovery for themselves, such as designing a paper aeroplane that will fly in a loop. They want to see their pupils' sense of accomplishment when they overcome their fear to climb to the top of the gym apparatus, or the pride on their faces when they score a goal wearing the school colours, or when they play an instrument and perform on stage in front of the school for the first time.

Primary school children are not little angels, though — and are far from innocent, either. The behavioural and emotional issues that arise with young children in primary schools can be every bit as complex and challenging as those found with teenagers in a secondary school. Do not think that life teaching in a primary school is idyllic — the healthy rattle and hum of even the friendliest primary school can occasionally become fractious and prompt you to feel claustrophobic.

But the joys described above can be very real, and primary school teachers can look forward to them more or less every day of the week. Such a prospect makes teaching in a primary school a very appealing, exciting and rewarding prospect for anyone with creativity, energy and empathy for young children.

Secondary

Schooling in the UK, to varying degrees, becomes more specialised and conformist as children get older and progress through the system. The apparent freedom and flexibility of nursery and primary schools, with their broad, mixed, child-centred structure and curriculum is replaced by a much more regimented system. Scottish secondary schooling is noted for the broader range of subjects studied as students get towards the end of their school careers, but the principle remains that secondary schools are characterised by the need to organise time and resources efficiently, so that children and teachers move about the school from room to room, subject to subject, according to a strict timetable with a defined agenda about what is to be taught and what is to be learned. On the other hand, it's the variety and pace of the secondary school day that appeals to many.

Charlotte Hopperton teaches geography:

> *"As much as I do genuinely adore smaller and younger children, there is something about being with the same 30 children from 9a.m. until 3.30p.m. that just does not appeal to me. I enjoy the constant rolling pace of secondary school teaching, and that I am expected to teach at different levels for different topics all in the same day."*

At secondary level, there is relatively little flexibility or time for young people to explore and discover things in the way they might have done more freely in nursery and primary school. In secondary education, children have a syllabus for a subject and a different teacher specialised in teaching each one.

Many people are attracted to secondary teaching simply because they really like and get on with young people. To many of us, teenagers might represent a seething mass of unbridled hormonal eruption. But some people really have a natural affinity and connection with young people. They love the idea, and the reality, of working with and assisting the personal, social, emotional and educational development of people of this age group. Some people really thrive on the challenges of motivating moody or disaffected teenagers, using charm and wit to get them on side long enough to spark an interest that they will then nurture and sustain.

Of course, most teaching in any school is unproblematic, and this allows teachers to focus on the reasons why many, if not most, of them came into teaching in the first place – the love of their subject and the passion they have for communicating it to their pupils and students.

If you have loved science at school and have gone on to study, for example, chemistry at degree level, you may have found you don't want to give it up. If perhaps research wasn't your thing, or there weren't appropriate opportunities to work in the particular industrial or commercial areas of interest, you could do worse than deciding that a working life enthusing others about the subject you love is a great way to make a living. If that's where you are right now, you need not apologise. Passionate obsessives are very welcome in teaching – not least because we can all recognise that the consummate single-mindedness of such people can be very charming.

And don't think that it is futile reproducing generations of unemployable chemists who end up in schools teaching another generation of the same – education doesn't work like that. If you have a passion for chemistry, and go on to become a teacher and motivate that passion in others, you may find that the youngsters you have taught go to on to take your subject into realms you would not have dreamed of – not only researchers, pharmacists and doctors, but into a wide variety of industrial, commercial and engineering careers in energy, food, pharmaceuticals, mining and manufacturing with applications you and they could not possibly have thought of at the time you were teaching them.

Secondary schools are organised a bit more like businesses in that they have departments where teachers are part of a specialist team within a management hierarchy. As a secondary school teacher, you will more than likely have a line manager who is the head of department or deputy head in a large department in a large school. This is in addition to the overall school management hierarchy that will include the head teacher and deputy and assistant heads.

Most secondary schools will average around 1,000–1,200 students, with some being considerably larger. Some departments, such as English, maths and science, will contain a large team of colleagues, where you may find not only your professional life but your social life centred. For subjects such as business studies or psychology, you may find there are only a handful of teachers in a small department and you'll need to reach out to other colleagues across the school for professional support, coaching and mentoring, let alone a social network.

Secondary school classrooms, as you'll probably remember from your own experience, are generally arranged so that classes sit in organised formations, often in rows of chairs and tables so that the mediation between a teacher and the class is largely regulated and overseen by the teacher themselves. Of course, this will not be the case in all schools, nor indeed for subjects such as PE, dance, drama and so on. Even in science subjects, the practical necessities of experiments in laboratories require different arrangements.

Once again, your choice of a teaching career needs to take full account of the relative constraints imposed on your working environment. If you are not good at organising people and practical resources effectively within tight timescales or confined spaces such as classrooms, labs or gymnasia, then teaching in a secondary school may not be for you.

While secondary teachers with departmental or pastoral responsibility will probably get fewer contact hours than their colleagues in nursery and primary education, they often have more onerous tasks in marking and preparation. A primary school teacher might have 30 exercise books with stories of 25–50 words in length if they are teaching children in Year 1, 2 or 3. Even with able children in Year 5 or 6, children's stories or essays are unlikely to be much longer than 400–500 words or so. In contrast, a secondary English, arts or humanities teacher might be reading, marking and commenting in detail on essays of up to five or six times that length, especially if they are teaching the subject to A level. The marking regime will also be much more onerous too, requiring detailed comments and in-depth feedback.

So, as a secondary teacher, the nature of your interaction with your students will be specialised and very focused. However, sometimes it is the nature of personality and character encountered in pupils of this age and maturity that is the fascination for some.

Chris Hildrew is an English and media teacher and a deputy head at a secondary school in Somerset:

> *"The reason I went into secondary rather than primary is that in the latter, children are children at the start and the end of the process. In secondary, they start as children and leave as adults, and that is what makes it so special to me. The associated challenges — the onset of puberty, their gradually increased independence (though the desire for and ability to handle it are not always matched . . .), the change in hormones, and coming to terms with an adult understanding of the world — for me all trump the love of a subject that is the driver towards secondary teacher training for most."*

Teenagers provide some challenges that are, of course, quite distinct from younger children. They are much more likely to engage you in conversation that is adult-like, mature and often sophisticated in nature. They are also less likely to be in awe of your authority in the way some young children clearly are; not that they are more likely to challenge that authority in a disruptive or negative way (younger children can also be extremely effective at doing that when they have a mind to) but you will find that students at secondary school will regularly express themselves in ways that do not necessarily show deference to your position as a teacher.

If you want to be a secondary teacher, you will need to understand and have sympathy for the way some teenagers behave, often precociously, and the way they express themselves, often bombastically, towards you and towards each other. Many people find this a real challenge to their nerves as much as their self-esteem, and perceive teenagers to be constantly challenging their authority. That is almost always not the case and is more usually a tactic young people use for attracting attention, although they may be using bizarre methods to do so.

However, in a context where the school atmosphere is safe and secure, and the emphasis is on achievement, teachers and their students can strike up very productive partnerships, where young people can form interactive and communicative working relationships that are highly conducive to teaching and learning. Indeed, many of the people who go into secondary teaching do so because they say they thoroughly enjoy the banter and the relationships one can have with teenage children, and how they can use the particular quality of that relationship to motivate them to engage with education in general and their subject in particular.

As with all phases of education, it is important to get a real sense of what it is really like by volunteering for an extended period in a school before applying for teacher training. Sometimes, teachers find that by volunteering in a primary school, it convinces them that they really want to be teachers — but definitely not in the primary sector!

As a secondary teacher, you will need a temperament that is pre-disposed to empathy, patience and tenacity, and you will need to be someone who can cope with the idea that your "to do" list will never be empty.

Many secondary teachers, however, will use an appropriate range of these tactics to form a general strategy of relationship-building that engages their students in the educational process. Teaching, one must always remember, is by definition an intimate engagement with some of the deepest motives that drive a young person's ambition and self-esteem. Good secondary teachers understand this possibly better than anyone, which is perhaps why so many get enormous satisfaction from their work.

Reflections from the newteachersblogger – newteachersblog.wordpress.com

What's the problem with inappropriate relationships?

News that a teacher and a student had a relationship may have come as a shock to many, particularly as the teacher is twice the age of his former pupil. But people of a certain age — those schooled in the 1970s and 1980s, for example — may be able to recall a variety of teacher–student flirtations, liaisons and even relationships that, while never approved of, didn't seem to shock then in the way that they do now.

These are tricky issues to raise, let alone discuss, so let me preface my comments by saying that any teacher who has a relationship with a student of whatever age is not only breaching the trust that lies at the heart of any professional–client relationship, but is also breaking the law. In my view, it's wrong.

However, attitudes and values change over time. The law that forbids teachers having any kind of "inappropriate relationship" with a pupil at the same school only came into force in 2003.

In contrast, three decades ago a teacher in the North East of England and a 15-year-old pupil began a relationship that was consummated by intercourse only when the pupil reached 16 and even then with the consent of her parents. Their later marriage bore a number of children and lasted more than 25 years.

Later, there was the celebrated case of the former Chief Inspector of Schools Chris Woodhead, who described a long-term relationship with one of his students as "educative". It lasted some years, and both he and she are unapologetic about it to this day.

A teacher doing today what Chris Woodhead did can expect summary dismissal and prosecution under the Sexual Offences Act. But the existing law does raise some interesting issues. For example, a teacher having a relationship with a student above the age of consent would neither necessarily be dismissed nor criminally convicted if the teacher and student were at different schools.

Is that no longer a "breach of trust"? No longer a "sexual offence"?

Are the issues more or less complex if the teacher is closer in age to the student? Not only is it conceivable that 22- or 23-year-old teachers might be the object of attraction to 16-, 17- and 18-year-old students, or vice versa, but it is extremely likely. Secondary schools up and down the country are chock full of both. Instances of teacher–student fraternisation are rare, but the opportunities are not.

Is there one of us who at some time in our own school days didn't have an irresistible crush on one of our teachers? How many of us, with hand on heart, can say that we would never have seized an opportunity, had it arisen, to take advantage of a situation to sneak a kiss with the teacher who was the object of our desires, on those occasions that lent themselves to sociability, fraternity and intimacy, such as residential field trips or overseas excursions? And if we had, would we have seen ourselves as the victim of a manipulative adult sexual predator?

I am not suggesting that students are the sexual predators or that teachers are the victims. I am convinced that the vast majority of such encounters will end with feelings of guilt, anger and loss of trust on the part of the student – although I do believe that those feelings will be intensified by the overbearing condemnation and judgement of others.

But in my view, vulnerability runs in both directions. A young teacher, particularly one attractive to students, can be the object of intense and perhaps sustained attention from a determined and charming admirer. If the teacher is inexperienced and perhaps immature, they too can be susceptible. Such a teacher may well be new to the school and even to the area, perhaps lonely and finding it difficult to make friends of a similar age. They may in such circumstances allow themselves to accept friendly, flattering, or even flirtatious approaches by sociable, seemingly "mature" students.

In such scenarios, temptation (let alone hormones) start to cloud better judgement.

But this is where a teacher's professional values should take over. If they do not, a teacher runs the risk of losing their personal reputation and their professional career. An understanding of appropriate conduct and professional values is not instantly awarded at the same time as Qualified Teacher Status.

No profession is immune from potential encounters, especially not one where the nature of the professional practice is based on social interaction, close physical proximity and appropriate degrees of intimacy. Being able to motivate, engage and inspire students often relies on this.

This is where the support, mentoring and good counsel from experienced and mature colleagues is both essential and invaluable. Teaching is a collegial profession, and the communication and counselling skills that experienced teachers acquire over a long career can guide and support not just the professional but the personal and pastoral needs of new, young teachers.

Let us not kid ourselves that the issues surrounding the way personal and professional relationships develop, particularly between young people of a similar age, are ever clear-cut. However stringently we may try to enforce safeguarding procedures, professional codes of conduct, or indeed the law, young people, both students and teachers, need support and good counsel as well as protection.

PART 2
Routes to qualifying

4

Choosing the best route for you

These days, there are a variety of routes by which you can qualify as a teacher. These include a range of university-based courses and, in England, the employment-based routes that allow you to learn on the job and earn a salary while you are doing it.

All the routes described in the next few chapters involve what is called initial teacher training (ITT) and they all include acquisition of Qualified Teacher Status (QTS). The standard of training, the preparation you receive to be a teacher and the professional rigour of the various courses described are broadly comparable to each other, and all ITT institutions in England are inspected by Ofsted to try to ensure that. The next few chapters comprise an important part of this book, so consider them carefully as they will help you decide which route is most suited to your style of learning and your own personal needs.

All the routes involve substantial periods on the job — doing teaching practices (TPs) or placements in school — so there will be plenty of time at the chalkface, whichever route you choose. Some provide the opportunity for a slower, more considered rate of induction into the rattle and hum of schools and classrooms;

some will put you in front of a class from day one; while others will give you the opportunity to practise as well as study teaching and education in a slightly more academic and reflective way as part of the course. Some routes might even award you credits towards a master's degree by the end of it.

First, focus on the following considerations to inform your choice.

- **Your prior experience of working with children or young people:** do you have a previous career as a nursery worker, youth worker or relevant experience such as training young people in industry, retail or the military? Prior *work* experience is not essential to get on a course, but weighs heavily as an advantage to your application, particularly if it is relevant. These days, however, gaining prior *school* experience is essential (and we'll deal with how you can get that shortly).

- **Your own prior educational achievement and qualifications:** do you already have a degree or a higher degree in a specific subject? Or do you want to acquire a degree as part of the training course?

- **Your preference for early years, primary or secondary teaching:** and if it is secondary, whether you have a degree in a relevant National Curriculum subject and enough existing subject knowledge to teach it. For example, if you have a degree in history and Spanish, but you majored in history and minored in Spanish, you may need to top up your knowledge of Spanish if you intend to teach it, through a Subject Knowledge Enhancement course (more of that later).

- **Your personal financial circumstances:** is earning a salary crucial to you during training, or can you afford to take on the burden of an additional student loan, at least for the short term?

- **Your personal, family and geographical circumstances:** are you constrained by the responsibilities of caring for children or is travelling long distances impractical for you?

Once you have weighed up these, your next key decision is whether you want to take:

- **a university based teacher-training route**, or a

- **a school-based teacher-training route** (although these are not available in Scotland).

This decision may be informed by some of the earlier considerations. For example, let's say you live in rural Norfolk and you want to train to be a secondary teacher. Your first thought is doing a PGCE on a university-based course because you have a degree in biology. But you also have a couple of children of school age, so travelling long distances to a university in Norwich or Cambridge is not a realistic option. This is where doing a school-based course might open up opportunities for you. These tend to be run by smaller providers working in local school clusters, and you may find one within easy driving distance of your home.

Once you have decided whether to take a university-based course or a school-based course, you have further options:

- **a university-based undergraduate route:** gaining QTS as part of an undergraduate degree such as a three-year bachelor of arts or bachelor of science (known as BA or BSc with QTS), or the once-ubiquitous but now less common four-year Bachelor of Education (BEd) course;

- **a university-based postgraduate route:** gaining QTS as part of a one-year (or a two-year part-time) course when you already have a degree in a relevant subject.* In England, this route is known as the Postgraduate Certificate in Education (PGCE), and in Scotland as the Postgraduate Diploma in Education (PGDE);

- **a school-based postgraduate SCITT route:** gaining QTS at a School-Centred Initial Teacher Training (SCITT) provider. Sometimes,

---

* A "relevant subject" is one taught as part of the National Curriculum, although this can be interpreted quite widely. For example, astronomy is not a National Curriculum subject, but having studied it, you may have substantial subject knowledge of physics – a shortage subject in teaching. You may need to check with the provider to see whether your degree needs topping up with additional subject knowledge through an SKE course; more about this later.

but not always, a SCITT may be partnered with a local university that will award the professional qualification of PGCE as part of the training;

- **a school-based postgraduate School Direct route**: gaining QTS via this new, heavily government-sponsored route has the greatest expectation, but not a guarantee, that you will have a job at the end of it.

All of these routes will equip you adequately to teach and will confer the gold standard of QTS (or Teaching Qualification, TQ, in Scotland), although as indicated earlier, the school and employment-based routes are not available in Scotland, and teachers who qualified in England via those routes are not automatically recognised as fully qualified in the Scottish system.

Many people in teaching will have their preferences for a particular route and some will have fairly strong views about what they think is the best way to train. Don't take too much notice of them. You have to decide what is best for *you* once you have considered all the relevant information.

For more information, please visit the Get into Teaching website at www.education.gov.uk/teachroutes, or call their Teaching Line on 0800 389 2500.

Profile: Institute of Education, University of Reading

The Institute of Education (IoE) at the University of Reading is one of the leading providers of teacher training in the UK. The Institute moved to its new home in January 2012, at the University's original London Road campus. The site has had a multi-million-pound refurbishment to bring you the best in modern technology and teaching resources.

In addition to those who achieve awards at master's and PhD level, every year close to 500 of our students become newly qualified teachers (NQTs). The University has excellent partnership arrangements with more than 300 local schools, which employ the majority of our graduates. Graduates from the Institute have an excellent chance of finding employment – well over 90% of our NQTs found a teaching job last year. With pay scales to match other industries, job security, an excellent teacher's pension and better work–life balance, teaching is becoming one of the most sought-after professions of today.

We offer the **PGCE** Secondary and Primary, **BA (Ed)** and **School Direct**. All PGCE students also qualify for 60 **master's** credits as part of their course. Our undergraduate courses include the unique **BA in Theatre Arts Education and Deaf Studies (TAEDS)** and the **BA in Children's Development and Learning (CDL)**. Building on the success of our **Foundation degree**, we have become established as a major provider for **Early Years Teacher Status**.

Contact information:
Email: ioe@reading.ac.uk
Web: www.reading.ac.uk/education

Follow the IoE on:
Facebook: Ioereading
Twitter: UniRdg_IoE

Case study

Study for a doctorate at the University of Reading and join the top 1%

The Educational Doctorate (EdD) at the Institute of Education offers research training and career development to a range of professionals in broad areas relating to education.

By enabling students to reflect critically on their professional contexts as well as understand the values that inform practice, the key aim of the programme is to develop high standards of research that will be relevant to a range of professional careers. This is a five-year part-time programme leading to a doctoral award. It incorporates two years of structured taught modules, followed by three years spent on the research thesis. **With the taught modules taking place over three weekends per year in the first two years, the programme is specifically designed with working professionals in mind.**

What current students have to say:
"I am impressed with every aspect of [the programme]. The course is well planned and professionally run, the lecturers are friendly, approachable and helpful, and the work is genuinely interesting and relevant ... I feel that what I have read has already made an impact on how I view teaching."
(Fiona, third-year doctoral student)

When you become a student with us, you will be joining an institution that is in the top 1% of the world's universities, according to the Times Higher Education World University Rankings 2012. This position reflects our academic reputation and commitment to delivering an excellent all-round education. We have been an international university for more than a century, and continue to offer degrees that are highly regarded by employers throughout the world.

To find out more, please contact Dr Carol Fuller, EdD Programme Director:
c.l.fuller@reading.ac.uk
or visit our website:
www.reading.ac.uk/education/pg-research/ioe-edd.aspx

When to apply

For a full range of university-based undergraduate and postgraduate teacher training courses you can visit UCAS (Universities and Colleges Admissions Service) at www.ucas.com/how-it-all-works/teacher-training. You can apply to UCAS at any time between mid-October and the end of June each year. They will send your application to training providers that have vacancies one at a time in your order of preference.

However, if you are applying for primary and early years PGCE or PGDE courses, the deadline is usually much earlier, often in early December. This deadline does not apply to PGCE and PGDE courses for middle years, secondary, post-compulsory or further education teaching courses, but if they receive your application between October and June, they will send it only to training providers that still have vacancies. Some popular training providers will fill their places for some courses very early in the training cycle.

So, whatever phase you want to teach in, you should apply as early as possible, to give yourself the best chance of obtaining a place.

If UCAS receive your application after the end of June, they will not send it to training providers but enter it into the Clearing system.

For post-graduate training courses in:

- **England:** www.ucas.com/ucas-teacher-training

- **Scotland:** www.teachinginscotland.com

- **Wales:** www.teachertrainingcymru.org/home

- **Northern Ireland:** You should make applications directly to the universities and training providers, but you can get preliminary information from the General Teaching Council for Northern Ireland at www.gtcni.org.uk. Deadlines vary slightly between institutions, but all are in either November or December.

Part-time and modular PGCEs

In England, there are some ITT training providers that offer modular or flexible PGCE courses. These try to cater for the personal needs and circumstances of people with family or with caring responsibilities, for example, and are often ideally suited to those with substantial prior learning and work experience – the kind of people who may be able to cope with juggling a lot of balls at once.

The structure and content of modular and flexible courses, while meeting the same standards as PGCEs nationally, will vary enormously from one provider to another. These courses normally have several different start and finish dates, so you are not necessarily bound by the academic calendar. Providers offer both full-time and part-time study and maybe even some training by distance learning, usually blocks of study on specific subjects or topics.

You should discuss your particular needs and circumstances with providers before you apply. To find such a course near you, go to the UCAS teacher training website and search the course profiles.

Troops to teachers scheme

The government recently introduced a scheme to enable ex-service personnel without degrees to train as teachers.

The course, which lasts two years, is largely school based, with four days out of five being in the classroom, supported by a mentor in that school. The approach is similar to school- or employment-based routes into teaching for graduates. The fifth day is spent in university, learning theoretical aspects of teaching and education.

The course is open to all ranks and can be applied for within two years of leaving the military, either before or after. Bursaries are available.

For more information, you can visit: https://troopstoteachers.ctp.org.uk.

Subject Knowledge Enhancement (SKE) courses

If you intend to teach at secondary level, you will need to be sure that your degree is either in a National Curriculum subject, or it offers enough specialist subject knowledge to teach that subject at a standard up to and including GCSE and A level.

For example, perhaps you have a degree in pharmacy, but the idea of teaching science to youngsters sounds more exciting than standing behind a counter all day doling out prescriptions. While your degree will have had a very substantial chemistry content, it may be that your overall knowledge of chemistry needs topping up in order for it to be adequate to teach at secondary level.

Help is at hand in the form of Subject Knowledge Enhancement (SKE) courses. Depending on your degree and the assessed subject content, these courses can sometimes be quite short, perhaps the equivalent of a two to three weeks' study, although they may sometimes be longer, depending on whether your knowledge needs a quick top-up or a more substantial make-over. Once again, depending on the individual course, you may be able to do this all in one go as a full-time course, or spread it over a longer period studying part-time, possibly as evening classes or weekend sessions.

Currently, SKE courses are only available in the following "shortage" subjects:

- mathematics

- physics

- chemistry

- computer science

- MFL

- D&T.

However, the first thing you should do is apply for a course at your chosen ITT provider. If they consider you to have the qualities to be a good teacher, they may offer you a conditional place on the teacher-training course, subject to you completing an SKE course. The ITT course provider is the one who makes the assessment and the final decision on whether you need SKE.

If you are applying for a PGCE, you can indicate on your application form that you are interested in doing an SKE course. Bursaries are available for them, too. Once you have successfully completed one of these courses, you are expected to go straight on to an ITT course leading to QTS.

To find out more about SKE courses, you can visit www.education.gov.uk/get-into-teaching and search for "subject knowledge enhancement programme", or call and speak to one of the Teaching Line consultants on 0800 389 2500. You can find out more about what may be required of you and in what regions the courses are running.

From outside the UK?

If you studied and gained qualifications outside the UK and are wondering whether your school or university qualifications are equivalent, then you can consult the

National Academic Recognition Centre (NARIC).

They will be able to advise you on whether your qualifications are equivalent to GCSEs, A levels and UK degrees.

Similarly, if you qualified as a teacher outside the UK, you can consult NARIC on whether your teaching qualification is equivalent to QTS in the UK. If you are from an EU country, in most cases there is a reciprocal agreement to recognise qualifications – but check to be sure.

To find out more, visit the NARIC website at www.ecctis.co.uk/naric.

Literacy and numeracy skills tests

Applicants for all teacher-training courses – whether graduate or undergraduate, university- and school- or employment-based – must pass the literacy and numeracy professional skills tests before they begin their course.

These tests are in addition to the other entry requirements of GCSE grade C or above in English and mathematics. They are intended to ensure that teachers have the basic competence in literacy and numeracy to carry out their professional duties, rather than concerned with the content of English and maths as curriculum subjects.

These tests have often unnecessarily daunted many excellent trainee teachers – particularly those who have been put off by numbers or those who are dyslexic. They are hurdles that have to be overcome if you want to be a teacher and; as with everything else, the better you prepare, the easier you will find them and the more confident you will feel.

You must pass them within three attempts. If you are dyslexic or your first language is not English and you are worried about them, you may be eligible for extra time to take them – up to 25% – but you'll need to provide some documentary evidence.

The tests can be taken at 150 test centres around the country and are administered by a private company, currently Pearson Professional Centres (where driving theory tests are also taken). The first test is free, but if you need a re-take there is a fee.

The literacy test consists of exercises that test your spelling, grammar, punctuation and comprehension. It lasts 45 minutes, unless you are eligible for additional time or special arrangements.

The numeracy test consists of:

- **Mental arithmetic.** This is an audio test heard through headphones. It includes mental calculations on time, fractions, percentages, measurements and conversions. You can't use a calculator for the mental section.

- **On-screen questions.** This will test your ability to interpret and use written data on such things as trends, comparisons and interpreting information.

- **Written arithmetic problems.** These cover topics such as time, money, proportion and ratio, percentages, fractions and decimals, measurements of distance and area, conversions from one currency to another and from fractions to decimals or percentages, averages and using simple formulae.

The numeracy test lasts about 50 minutes unless you are eligible for additional time.

As mentioned above, a lot of trainees get terribly worked up about these tests. The fact that the government recently made passing them compulsory before starting a course may have intensified that feeling for many. If it's any consolation, more than 98% of people pass them and there's minimal statistical variation with age, gender, ethnicity, disability or whether English is your first language or not. So don't worry about them. You'll have bigger challenges than these once you start teaching in practice!

For more information, including how to register and apply for skills tests, take a look at:

www.education.gov.uk/get-into-teaching/apply-for-teacher-training/skills-tests

How will I be assessed?

In England, all trainees of whatever route are assessed by the Teachers' Standards that have been drawn up by the DfE. These set out the expectations as to the skills, knowledge, attributes and qualities that teachers must show they have acquired by the time they complete their training. Here is a summary of them.

Part one

- Set high expectations that inspire, motivate and challenge pupils.

- Promote good progress and outcomes by pupils.

- Demonstrate good subject and curriculum knowledge.

- Plan and teach well-structured lessons.

- Adapt teaching to respond to the strengths and needs of all pupils.

- Make accurate and productive use of assessment.

- Manage behaviour effectively to ensure a good and safe learning environment.

- Fulfil wider professional responsibilities.

Part two

A teacher is expected to demonstrate consistently high standards of personal and professional conduct . . . throughout their career.

Teachers must have proper and professional regard for the ethos, policies and practices of the school in which they teach, and maintain high standards in their own attendance and punctuality.

Teachers must have an understanding of, and always act within, the statutory frameworks that set out their professional duties and responsibilities.

Teachers uphold public trust in the profession and maintain high standards of ethics and behaviour, within and outside school, by:

- treating pupils with dignity, building relationships rooted in mutual respect, and at all times observing proper boundaries appropriate to a teacher's professional position

- showing tolerance of and respect for the rights of others

- not undermining fundamental British values, including democracy, the rule of law, individual liberty and mutual respect, and tolerance of those with different faiths and beliefs

- ensuring that personal beliefs are not expressed in ways that exploit pupils' vulnerability or might lead them to break the law.

Profile: Nottingham Trent University

NOTTINGHAM
TRENT UNIVERSITY

From our launch in 1960, we have successfully grown into one of the UK's leading providers of education-related and teacher-training courses. The wealth of experience gained over the past five decades has enabled us to create a diverse range of courses offering you the opportunity to train to be a teacher or study education in its widest context. We undertake award-winning, pioneering research that informs government policy, and a number of our staff contribute to national bodies, shaping the future of UK education.

Teacher-training courses

We are a highly regarded centre for training teachers for primary and secondary schools and further education colleges. Given our extensive partnership arrangements with local schools and colleges, trainees benefit from the expertise and guidance of practising teachers as well as from university tutors.

Trainee teachers develop good subject knowledge and gain a range of experiences in the classroom and other settings, giving them a wider understanding of children's learning. This preparation makes them very attractive to schools, and we are consistently above the national average for the number of our students in teaching roles within a year of graduating (National College for Teaching and Leadership data, February 2012).

Professional and career development courses

For those already working in education who want to gain further academic qualifications and enhance their career development, we have a range of courses that offer flexible progression routes with a variety of entry and exit points, enabling students to work through different levels at their own pace.

Whether you are looking for a short course to improve your subject knowledge, a specialist course to improve your teaching practice, or a master's examining wider education issues, our professional courses can give your career the boost you are looking for.

Beyond studying

Studying at NTU is about more than just your course. There are plenty of opportunities to get involved in different activities including sport and fitness, and a diverse and eclectic mix of societies who also welcome postgraduate students for their experience and maturity.

Most of our courses are based on our Clifton campus (D&T and Engineering are studied at our City site), an attractive self-contained greenfield site located on the outskirts of Nottingham.

Clifton boasts excellent transportation links, newly extended sports facilities, a convenience store, refectory and the Point Bar – a popular meeting point for our students.

Find out more

Talk to our tutors, find out about modules and methods of study, and take a look around our campuses on an open day.

Find out more now at www.ntu.ac.uk/edu.

Contact us

School of Education
Nottingham Trent University
Clifton Lane
Nottingham
NG11 8NS
Tel: +44 (0)115 941 8418
Teacher training courses: edu.ite-enquiries@ntu.ac.uk
Graduate and Professional courses: edu.cpd@ntu.ac.uk

Case study

Elizabeth Clarson, BA (Hons) Primary Education, Nottingham Trent University

Elizabeth found that the degree on offer at Nottingham Trent (NTU) was practical and prestigious with plenty of potential.

NTU was my ideal choice due to its great reputation, opportunities available throughout the four-year course, and that it was local. The primary education course particularly appealed to me because of the amount of time that the students seemed to be on placements within schools. I was keen to choose a course that would give me the practical classroom experience to support the learning from university-based sessions.

I have found that there is a really friendly and supportive environment at NTU, which has allowed me to get fully involved in my course as well as lots of other activities within the School of Education, ranging from fundraising to working as an ambassador. The academic staff are really supportive and approachable, allowing good relationships to be developed with the students. This allows us to feel supported at every step throughout the four years of the course, and beyond that into our future teaching careers.

The course covers all areas of children's learning, including the background theories, the subject knowledge and the techniques for application within the classroom. There are also opportunities for further involvement such as the Take One Picture project with the National Gallery, residential trips in the UK, and the special placement opportunity in Year Three, where students get the chance to travel the world and experience education in different contexts. There are specialist classrooms where hands-on sessions are taught such as art, D&T and science. ICT rooms are also available across the campus for teaching and private study.

This course has allowed me to develop my skills as a teacher as well as giving me opportunities to work alongside others to develop my team work and people management skills. This will be valuable to me in the future, particularly in roles of responsibility within schools. On completion of my course, my target is to get a job as a teacher within the Nottinghamshire area and eventually complete a master's degree in Education. My ultimate aim would be to take up a management role within a school. This course is a fantastic starting point for a career in education as it allows access to a variety of opportunities while supporting individuals to develop into outstanding teachers.

Can I afford to train as a teacher?

Managing financially while training to be a teacher is an issue for everyone, but the implications vary from one person to the next. For example, if you have a family to support, a mortgage to pay and are coming from a well-paid, established career in the financial sector, assessing the risks of training to become a teacher might be more a lot more complex than if you are 18 or 19 years old, have just finished your A levels, are living at home with your parents and thinking of a doing an undergraduate teacher-training course at a local university.

Whatever your circumstances, unless you have a wealthy maiden aunt, you are unlikely to be well off during the period you are a student or training to be a teacher. You will have to manage a tight budget – although you may be used to that if you have come straight from a degree course. You may have to change your lifestyle for a while and miss out on some things that you have become used to – this will be especially true if you have come from a relatively well-paid job in industry or commerce. You may have to save for a year or more to build up a contingency fund or ask your family to make sacrifices, such as going without a holiday for a year.

While there are financial issues about training to teach, there are some positive things you should bear in mind.

- Remember why you want to be a teacher – yes, you may be unhappy in your current job or you love your degree subject so much you want to be a student for as long as possible, but it's probably because you are passionate about wanting to make a difference to other people's lives that is really driving your motivation. Remembering this will be important to sustain you through the period of your training.

- Being a student or a trainee doesn't last for ever – think of it as short-term financial pain for long-term gain in the quality of your working life.

- Once you get in to teaching, advancement compares favourably with many sectors. For example, government figures claim that teachers are twice as likely on average to be in management positions within three years of entering the profession, than graduates in other sectors. If you have come with experience in industry or commerce, you are in a good position to take best advantage of that.

- Even for new graduates, starting salaries in teaching are above the national average for graduate professions.

- Financial support is available for some trainees, particularly if you are a good graduate in a shortage subject – there are scholarships and tax-free bursaries that will help support you (see the section on "Training bursaries and scholarships", below).

Fees and loans

Tuition fees are charged for full-time teacher-training students and trainees in England and Wales, and these are currently £9,000 a year. However, they do vary considerably between one university and college ITT provider and another, and this is particularly true of SCITT providers, some of whom are not charging nearly that amount.

As you may already be aware, loans up to £9,000 are available to cover tuition fees in full and only have to be repaid once you have left university or teacher training and have started to earn over £21,000 a year. Maintenance loans to cover accommodation and other living costs are available but are means tested.

Training bursaries and scholarships

As a postgraduate trainee, depending on the degree subject and class you have, you could be eligible for support during your training, either with a tax-free bursary or a scholarship from a professional body.

Bursaries

Bursaries are available if you want to teach the following subjects in secondary schools:

- Maths, physics, chemistry and MFL: tax-free bursaries are available up to:

  ○ £20,000 for those with a first-class degree

  ○ £15,000 for those with a 2:i

  ○ £12,000 for those with a 2:ii

- English, geography, history, computer science, Latin, Greek, music, biology and design and technology: tax-free bursaries are available up to:

  ○ £9,000 for those with a first-class degree

  ○ £4,000 for those with a 2:i

If you want to teach maths as a specialist subject in a primary school, you could receive up to £11,000 with a first or £6,000 with a 2:i.

Scholarships from professional associations and bodies

Those with a 2:i or first in maths, physics, chemistry and computer science can also apply for a tax-free scholarship to train as a teacher from the relevant subject professional association or bodies.

- **Institute of Mathematics and its Applications (IMA):** www.ima.org.uk

- **London Mathematical Society (LMS):** www.lms.ac.uk

- **Royal Statistical Society (RSS):** www.rss.org.uk

- **Institute of Physics (IOP):** www.iop.org

- **Royal Society of Chemistry (RSC):** www.rsc.org/education

- **Chartered Institute for IT (BCS):** www.bcs.org

while more general details on funding for postgraduate training can be found at:

- www.education.gov.uk/teachpgfunding.

Starting salaries

As a new teacher on the main pay scale (at the time of writing in 2013), you will start on a minimum of:

- England and Wales: £21,588

- London fringe: £22,626

- Outer London: £25,117

- Inner London: £27,000.

Salaries are considerably more for teachers on the upper main scale, for experienced teachers and those on the leadership scale.

Teaching and learning responsibility payments (so-called TLRs) are paid in addition to the main pay scales, starting at £2,353 and rising to £12,393.

For more detail and up-to-date pay scales, see: www.education.gov.uk/teachsalaries.

5

University-based undergraduate routes: BA or BSc (QTS) and BEd

If you are the kind of person who likes to develop skills and digest knowledge at a pace that will allow reflection and consideration of all the various angles and dimensions of a complex profession such as teaching, then a three- (or even four-) year undergraduate degree course might be the best route for you.

As with the other routes, you will acquire QTS during your course, but this way you will gain an honours degree in a specialist subject or area of education in the process. These courses are often titled:

- BA (QTS) for Bachelor of Arts with Qualified Teacher Status, or

- BSc (QTS) for Bachelor of Science with Qualified Teacher Status, or

- BEd for Bachelor of Education (including QTS).

This route is probably the best for those people who have always known that they wanted to be teachers or who are sure that it is what they want to do, both now and as a long-term career, because it offers the opportunity to get both a degree and a teaching qualification within three or four years. Other routes may take longer – and in these days of increasing student loans and mounting debt, that may be an issue for you.

The undergraduate route might also suit people who are going to university for the first time and want to enjoy the pleasures and relatively relaxed atmosphere of student life. You will be mixing with people doing all kinds of other degrees and courses (there are relatively few teacher-training-only university colleges left now), so you will experience student life in all its diversity.

One of the many advantages of this route is that you have greater opportunity to experience a variety of school placements over an increasingly long period of time as your confidence and skill begins to build. Typically, you'll be placed in three or four different schools for between three and 12 weeks over the period of the course, often with varying social and ethnic backgrounds if you're lucky, so you'll feel like you're quite experienced by the end.

You'll also have quite a variety of modules – perhaps 16 to 18 different topics over the three years – and these days, most are assessed not by examination but by a mixture of formats. So for example it's quite typical that practically oriented courses such as teaching are assessed by coursework assignments ranging from 1,500–3,000 words that might include making resources for the classroom, preparing posters, audio-visuals and presentations. There may be just one or two longer written assignments such as a 5,000–8,000-word project or thesis towards the very end of the course.

Another thing to be said is that they offer a wider range of support for those initially lacking confidence. You'll not only have a school-based mentor (usually the teacher of the class that you're taking over) to support you with ideas and practical advice while you are on placement, but you'll also have a university tutor visiting every so often to see how you're getting on and to give you a little pep talk – and, if the worst comes to the worst, an extra shoulder to cry on!

Laura Bellars completed her BA (QTS) last year:

> *"One of the main reasons I chose this route into teaching was the length of the course. Three years seemed like an*

appropriate amount of time to experience teaching for myself and to develop my subject knowledge. If I had chosen the PGCE, however, I feel as if it would have been too intense, and I might have found the whole experience too stressful. Another reason was that as you progress through the course, you are given more independence, and this is true both of assignments and teaching practice."

The structure and content of a BEd course is broadly similar, though depending on the university provider, you might find a greater proportion of subject knowledge related to education topics. So the course could include a slightly greater number or proportion of modules such as "The Philosophy and Sociology of Education" or "Educational Theory and Practice", or slightly more content related to something such as "The role of play in child development", with a proportionally greater element of these modules going towards final degree classification.

Four-year BEd courses were the norm for undergraduate routes a few years ago, but are now becoming less common (and this is especially true in Scotland for those wanting to teach at secondary level). This is largely to do with the way government is influencing funding structures in teacher training and giving more emphasis to school-based routes, but it's also because students themselves — facing the prospect of paying off student loans — are tending to choose shorter courses rather than longer ones, where they feel the end result is going to be the same.

However, you can still find BEd courses being offered by many ITT providers across the country, although more are available for primary than secondary teaching. So if you want to focus a little more of your efforts on the academic study of teaching or just take that bit longer building your skills and confidence at a slower rate, then a three- or four-year BA (QTS) or BEd might be ideal for you.

Here are a couple of examples to give you an idea of both the structure and the content of undergraduate routes. For instance, Mike Lambert, a Principal Lecturer at the University of Wolverhampton, describes the BEd in Early Primary or Primary Education offered there:

"On our course, 'Early Primary' trainees (about one third of the annual cohort, so that's about 30–40 students) train to teach children aged 3–7. 'Primary' trainees (about two–

thirds of the annual cohort, about 60–70 students) train to teach children aged 5–11.

"The timetable for BEd trainees covers up to 35 weeks in the academic year.

"Trainees have four main teaching practice 'attachments' or 'placements' in the three years: one in Year 1 (five weeks); one in Year 2 (seven weeks); and two in Year 3 (five weeks and eight weeks).

"There is also other, shorter-term involvement in schools. Year 3 trainees have a one-week alternative educational placement, which trainees themselves choose and arrange. This could, for example, be in a museum, or zoo-based educational service, or an adventure centre, or in a pupil referral unit. Some trainees also choose to do an extra voluntary three-week placement in a special school at the end of their second year.

"In addition, trainees follow four or five university-based modules each year. Each module has two assessment components – these may be examinations, essays, presentations or tasks linked to school placements.

"Our BEd trainees complete a 'research methods' module in Year 2, leading to a research-based investigation in an educational setting in Year 3 – this is their 'dissertation', and gives Honours status to their degree."

Perhaps because of the length and structure of these courses, they tend to attract students who are aware of their relative inexperience and lack of academic knowledge. Laura Bellars again, summing up the pros and cons:

"For me, the pros of a BA (QTS) are first that the length of the course is adequate to develop subject knowledge and gain a lot of experience in school – which I believe suits all kinds of abilities – and there are regular audits of your subject knowledge in the core core subjects of English, mathematics and science. I also think the variety of teaching placements in *different schools is a real plus, particularly as they increase each year of the course. As for the cons: this route may be too long for some students, particularly if you already have very good subject knowledge."*

Paul Smalley, a Senior Lecturer from Edge Hill University, describes the BA (Hons) in Secondary Religious Education (RE) with QTS offered there. Edge Hill also has secondary BA (QTS) courses in modern languages, mathematics, English and sciences, though the course structure for those is broadly the same:

"Term starts in October and ends in July. The course is taught in modules — each is about 40 contact hours plus lots of individual study! Each year there is a professional studies module that includes up to 20 lectures and follow-up seminars, on average one a week. There is also a 'Teaching RE' module, with a different focus each year (planning, teaching, assessing).

"There are three or four Religious Education subject knowledge modules per year that cover the six major world faiths usually taught in high schools. Then a 'research methods' module in Year 2 to prepare for the School Improvement Study (which is an individual research project, like a short dissertation) in Year 3. All of these are examined by written assignments or a portfolio of 4,000-word equivalence — there are no exams!

"We place a lot of emphasis on experiential learning: many university sessions are designed to show good classroom teaching practice (interaction, group work, active learning) and we make good use of visits (to schools and religious places) and have lots of visitors (such as leading teachers and others from education and from the faith communities).

"Each year has a block school placement: In Year 1 this is usually undertaken in student pairs and is an initial introduction to schools — lots of guided observation with some team teaching and small group teaching, leading up to some whole-class solo teaching as appropriate to the individual needs of the student.

> "In Year 2, the focus is on students, planning and delivering schemes of work, predominantly on their own, but with some support from university tutors and school-based mentors. In Year 3, the focus is on consolidating their practice, particularly with regard to assessment and clearly demonstrating how well they meet the teaching standards in their final practice.

> "The time spent on placement varies slightly each year, and is between eight and 12 weeks. Students will have their placements in at least two and usually three schools of varying characteristics, as well as a number of additional day visits to schools to see particularly good practice. Over the three years, students are likely to spend over 150 days in school."

This is what the structure of the course looks like at Edge Hill; it is summarised in Table 3. While the structure will be similar elsewhere, the content may be very different.

Perhaps a distinctive feature of undergraduate courses is the demographic: BA and BSc (QTS) and BEd courses tend to attract students with relatively little full-time work experience. A large proportion, although certainly not all, come more or less straight from school, but this varies from university to university and from course to course.

However, such courses also attract people who are entering higher education through non-standard routes, perhaps completing an Access course after having left school many years earlier. Some have had a family and decided that they now want to return to work and do something fulfilling. Some universities, particularly those in large cities that were once polytechnics, have a strong reputation in recruiting students with such a profile.

This route tends to have much larger cohorts than for school-based routes, so on courses like this you'll probably have 100–150 other students in your year group and perhaps 400–500 on the course; so you'll have plenty of people with whom you can share similar problems and ideas, as well as socialise.

Many tutors feel that this kind of course is excellent for those people who "always knew they wanted to be teachers", and left school intending to pursue a career in teaching as soon as they could. As mentioned earlier, it provides a supportive environment for those who feel their confidence and skills need building up more slowly.

Table 3. Structure of BA (QTS) in Secondary RE at Edge Hill University

Stage	Module							
	Personal and Professional Conduct	Teaching Skills	Subject study	Subject Study: Eastern stream	Subject study: Scripture stream	Subject study: Theology stream	Research	Total credits
Year 1 (Level 4)	20 credits	Principles, Planning and Pedagogy in RE (20 credits)	Beginning the Study of Religion (20 credits)	Hindu Dharma (20 credits)	Islam (20 credits)	History of Christian Thought and Culture (20 credits)		120
Year 2 (Level 5) 20 credits	Creative Medium-Term Planning and Teaching in RE (20 credits)		Buddhist Dharma (20 credits)	Judaism (20 credits)	Old Testament Theology (20 credits)	Research Methods (20 credits)		120
Year 3 (Level 6)	20 credits	Classroom Assessment and Target-setting Skills in RE (20 credits)		Eastern Dharma: Sikhism and Jainism (20 credits)	New Testament Criticism (20 credits)	Religion in the Twenty-first Century (20 credits)	School Improvement Study in RE (20 credits)	120
Programme totals	60 credits	60 credits			200 credits		40 credits	360

Table reprinted with the permission of Paul Smalley from Edge Hill University

95

Andreana Panayi, a recent graduate of a three-year BEd from the University of Hertfordshire, says just that:

"I felt that a three-year full-time course would benefit me as it would give me a longer period of time to gain knowledge and experience in the theory and pedagogy side of teaching. As I decided to go down the primary route, I believed a BEd would be better (as opposed to a subject degree plus PGCE), as it focuses more on teaching rather than a single subject.

"I was at university five days a week for three years and during that time I completed three different school placements — one a year. In Year 1 the placement lasted eight weeks and in Years 2 and 3 it was for nine weeks. Each of these placements was at a different school, in different areas and in different year groups.

"On each placement I was allocated a mentor (usually the class teacher) and a university tutor. My mentor would observe and grade me once a week and my university tutor would observe and grade me twice, once at the beginning and once at the end of my placement.

"My course did not require me to take exams. However, I was required to pass modules each term in order to progress to the next year. The modules all consisted of written assignments that would be marked and classified, and it would be these that would lead to my final degree result.

"Three years, although quite intense, was a good time scale for me to develop knowledge, confidence and experience. The BEd route allowed me to develop subject knowledge as well as pedagogy, and the placements meant I could experience different year groups. It catered for a range of personalities and abilities and I preferred the assignment-based assessments as I never perform well in exam situations.

"The fact it was full-time meant that it was hard to have a job and earn money unless you were willing to work seven days *a week! The placements took up a lot of the year, and so the assignments were squeezed into quite a short period of time. I felt well prepared in terms of my knowledge (although more time could have been put in to learning the administrative side of teaching, such as levelling, report-writing, target-setting etc.), but I don't think you are ever fully prepared until you actually start teaching.*

"The general quality of university teaching was really good. It was inspiring and catered for different needs and abilities. I really enjoyed it, felt it prepared me well and would most definitely recommend it."

You can search the UCAS site for undergraduate ITT courses in your area and by subject (www.search.ucas.com) or for other information about this route, see www.education.gov.uk/get-into-teaching/teacher-training-options/university-based-training/undergraduate-itt.

6

University-based postgraduate routes: PGCE or PGDE and PGDipEd

If you already have a degree and want to balance your exposure to school with continued interest in study and the measured support of a university, then the one-year PGCE or the less common Professional Graduate Diploma in Education (PGDipEd) in England or the PGDE in Scotland may be for you.

This postgraduate route will suit people who already have very good subject knowledge but perhaps don't feel completely confident about being thrown in at the deep end. It offers a graduated introduction to the classroom the support of mentors and tutors until you develop the confidence to stand on your own two feet in front of a class of children.

However, it is a fast-paced and intense course – lasting from September to late June or July – and you'll need to be the kind of person who can cope with that pressure, or at least get up to speed very quickly. The complexity and challenge of being a teacher will be introduced to you fairly quickly, but you will find the year extremely rewarding because the university work and the school placements are structured in a way that will swiftly build your confidence. The course will allow time for reflection, observation of other good teachers and an integration of educational theory with teaching practice.

Profile: Liverpool Hope University

Liverpool Hope
University

Why choose a graduate route into teaching at Liverpool Hope University?

Liverpool Hope is a unique university by virtue of its rich and distinctive nineteenth-century foundations. Its long and proud history of preparing teachers dates from 1844, when it began to educate teachers in the Christian tradition for the rapidly growing communities of Liverpool and the wider North West region. Many of Liverpool Hope's graduate teachers hold distinguished careers around the country, and indeed elsewhere in the world.

The University's mission is to provide a well-rounded education for the whole person, which is why programmes are considered to be initial teacher education and not merely training. We offer two routes into teaching – School Direct and the PGCE route. All our secondary subjects are taught through the PGCE pathway, and secondary and primary are School Direct courses.

Liverpool Hope University has well-established and powerful partnerships with primary and secondary schools throughout Greater Merseyside, as well as parts of Lancashire, Cheshire and Greater Manchester. Working closely with the University, these schools will encourage, challenge and support you so that your work-based learning is an integral and valuable part of your course. It is important that you not only develop the skills, knowledge and understanding to be competent in the classroom but that you are aware of the bigger picture of the school, community and region in which you are working.

As well as having a holistic experience of working in schools, Liverpool Hope wants you to read and understand research that informs the practice of supporting children in their learning and personal development. This is why the PGCE at Liverpool Hope University is a postgraduate course studied and assessed at master's level. The best teachers are reflective practitioners, grounded in the skills of evidence-based practice, developed through programmes such as the PGCE at Hope that go beyond a "tips for teachers" approach.

Many of Liverpool Hope's student teachers have taken advantage of opportunities to participate in school-based experiences in Europe, the USA and the Middle East. Others, who wish to make their careers in faith-based schools, have opted to pursue courses that help them to prepare for such opportunities.

As well as being experienced practitioners with many years spent in classrooms, most tutors at Liverpool Hope are also academic specialists engaged in research. It is often possible for students to collaborate with tutors on their research projects.

For further information, please contact the Student Recruitment Team on +44 (0)151 291 3111 or email enquiry@hope.ac.uk.

Full details of all Liverpool Hope University's programmes can also be found on their website at www.hope.ac.uk. Here you will also find specific entry criteria and lots of other helpful information about finance and life as a student at Hope.

Case study

Former Liverpool Hope University student, Andrew Hall, gives us an insight into his degree and its intense workload which is complemented by excellent support and pastoral care.

"…being a teacher is a vocation and one which will challenge you on a daily basis."

Being able to reflect on your own practice is an integral part of the PGCE, and looking back on my own time on the course enables me to see how much I have developed. Liverpool Hope University provide excellent support both in terms of practical knowledge to be used in the classroom and a pastoral support which caters for the needs of each individual trainee. The course provides you with many opportunities to develop as a young professional. The standards that Hope expect are very high and you will be challenged from your very first day.

Being on placement gives you an insight into the day-to-day practice of a classroom teacher, as well as giving you the opportunity to put into practice the skills and knowledge learnt during lectures and seminars. At first, it was a daunting prospect, getting up in front of a class for the first time. Yet the foundations built through the help of the tutors enable you to develop and grow as a trainee teacher.

For me, being a teacher is a vocation and one which will challenge you on a daily basis. Do not enter the profession for an easy ride because I can guarantee there are no short cuts to be taken. Hard work and dedication are essential in order to succeed. Be organised and be professional at all times and the rewards you will receive from teaching will be unrivalled. Would I change the late nights planning and preparing lessons? Not a chance.

The PGCE route may also suit people who have been very happy studying a particular subject at a particular university and want to extend that period, combining it with a fledgling interest in teaching. For some, the discovery that they can spend their working day talking about the subject they love is a fantastic revelation. Your work is *fun* ... how cool is that!

Of course, there are some who discover that, while they have a passion for their subject, teaching is not for them, and they have just lost a year of their earning potential and perhaps added more to their student debt ... Just put it down to experience – that's life.

But having done a PGCE, many go on to find that even what appeared to be a wasted year has delivered some unexpected benefits, such as improved communication and people skills, which are great assets for any career move.

PGCE courses are available in early years, primary and secondary phases. As with all postgraduate routes, in order to apply to train as a teacher through a PGCE route, you must have a UK undergraduate degree or a recognised equivalent qualification, GCSE grade C or above in English and mathematics and, if you are applying to teach primary or at Key Stage 2–3 (7–14 years old), you must also have a science subject at grade C or above.

If for example, you go to a large university for a secondary course, Manchester or the Institute of Education (IOE) in London, for instance, you will find that there may be a PGCE cohort of some hundreds of students. Even the subject cohorts are large enough for you to find yourself in a group of at least 15–20 people. Some people find having a large group of other trainees all studying the same subject very supportive and stimulating. This is how Warren Valentine, who did a PGCE in history, found life at the IOE:

> *"My history cohort within the course has 18 very different people. They are all amazing, and having this support network to bounce ideas off and socialise with has been important in maintaining morale. We support each other with our weaknesses, whether that be subject knowledge, creativity or how academic you are (the MA assignments for example)."*

Profile: Institute of Education

Initial Teacher Education at the Institute of Education, University of London

The Institute of Education (IOE) is the only college of the University of London dedicated entirely to education and related areas of social science. We have a reputation for excellence, expertise and innovation that stretches across the world. Each year we train almost 2,000 aspiring teachers across a range of programmes.

A range of opportunities

We offer initial teacher education (ITE) at primary, secondary and post-compulsory (lifelong learning) level and have a range of different training options to suit your aspirations and previous experience:

- PGCE Primary to teach pupils aged 5–11, full-time or part-time routes

- PGCE Secondary to teach pupils aged 11–16 or 14–19, in 17 subject specialisms

- PGCE Post-Compulsory to teach learners aged 16+ (including adults), with full-time pre-service and part-time pre- or in-service routes, plus the option to take a generic route or specialise in either literacy and English for speakers of other languages (ESOL) or mathematics with numeracy

- School Direct salaried or training routes at primary or secondary levels

- Teach First

- Assessment Only.

Outstanding teacher training

In the Newly Qualified Teachers' Survey 2013, over 90% of IOE NQTs rated their training as good or very good. In our most recent Ofsted inspection, all our ITE programmes were rated as outstanding.

Unrivalled school partnerships

We work with more than 600 partnership schools and colleges in London, the East and the South East of England to place students from all our ITE routes.

Great career prospects

Our graduates are highly sought-after in schools and colleges throughout the UK, and with well over 10,000 teachers trained by the IOE in the last decade, you don't have to go far in teaching to meet other IOE alumni.

Many of our graduates are offered positions in the schools where their teaching practice takes place. Within six months, 93% per cent of ITE students who graduated in 2011–12 had obtained teaching positions in the UK and overseas. We also organise events to support our ITE students in finding employment.

Case study

Bayzid Ahmed, PGCE Secondary Computer Science with ICT

Bayzid followed the advice of former PGCE students and went to the IOE – and he found the quality of advice from former teachers on the course invaluable to his own practice.

"The reason I chose IOE, first and foremost, is because of the reputation. I considered various other institutions out there and asked people who have done the PGCE, and they came back to me and said, 'It's got to be at the IOE.' The best thing about training here were the lectures on assessment techniques, teaching strategies and behaviour management. When former teachers and experts talk about what strategies are out there, what you need to do, it's uplifting; it does help you, especially when you put it into practice. Throughout the course, it's made me realise how confident I've become. I feel I'm ready for anything now."

For more information about initial teacher training at the IOE, visit www.ioe.ac.uk/ITT

Apart from the focus on subject or phase knowledge, all providers will have a core structure of lectures and seminars that are related to a programme of wider professional and general teaching studies shared with the whole cohort – which could be up to 400 or 500 in large universities, although the average will be around 150, particularly on primary courses.

Even with an intense course such as the PGCE, you will have experience of at least two and usually three very different schools, and your exposure to the classroom will be gradually built up but you will feel supported by both a university tutor and a school mentor. Many PGCE trainees comment favourably on the access to dedicated professional and academic support that is provided by university tutors throughout the year. They work as teams, and as former classroom teachers themselves, are ideally placed to provide high-quality academic reflection that supports practical, professional development of your skills.

Similarly, in school, many trainees feel the complementary experience of university and school really works. Warren found that:

> "A PGCE gives a good grounding in testing the effectiveness of subject teaching. It has allowed me to approach my school's

way of doing things with a healthy questioning attitude. I feel that I have benefited from the way my first school does things, which also gave me a grounding in the 'real world' in a way that the university does not. But the university teaching has also reminded me of the core direction we should be pulling in, rather than descending into a purely pragmatic attitude, which I might otherwise do. I have spent a lot of time with a history specialist at university, which has been brilliant for my development. "

An academic expectation is embedded in the PGCE. If you don't find the mix of theory and practice interesting, don't think it's essential to becoming a teacher, or don't want to take this aspect of teachers' professionalism seriously, then a PGCE is probably not for you.

The PGCE structure does often reveal, however, that there is more than one type of good teacher. Dr Andy Howes teaches on the Secondary PGCE at Manchester University:

"There is always a small number of trainees who find that they excel in one of their school placements, while only just managing to meet the QTS standards in the other with all the support and guidance available. This reflects the fact that there is more than one type of good teacher, but that good teachers are not necessarily good in all school contexts. The PGCE offers the opportunity to develop as a good teacher while also learning about the type of institutional context that will be conducive to further development.

"Then there is another group of trainees who take time to find their feet in the classroom and make the crucial transition from student to teacher. Structured in the way it is, the PGCE allows these trainees to move on through the course, leaving their early difficult classroom experiences behind them. "

This is an important point, reinforced and well illustrated by Tom Jordan, who did a PGCE in business education at Sheffield Hallam:

"I found my two placements both challenging in different ways, but on reflection I feel this benefited my experience greatly. Due to the small size of business departments, it can sometimes mean that the success or failure of a placement can be based on one person's opinions. I found this on my first placement where I was put on 'cause for concern'.

"Although I understood that my observations could have gone better, I felt as though I was in a tough situation at an extremely challenging school. But due to the small department there it was essentially the business teacher's word against mine. After help from my university mentor and the support I got from another student I was paired with, I passed the placement.

"On my second placement, however, I was in a department of five teachers and found this a great source of resources and advice. The placement went really well."

PGCE and PGDE courses are easily found at most universities across the UK (PGDipED courses are slightly less common), and their structure and content are broadly similar. However, there will be some differences, given secondary subject content and the fact that primary PGCE students normally spend around 18 weeks in school while their secondary counterparts will have slightly longer, up to 24 weeks.

It's important that you find as much detail as you can about the course structure of a particular provider before making a final decision, so compare the information on websites and ask specific questions of their recruitment offices, particularly if you might need to top up your subject knowledge or want to have the flexibility of a two-year part-time PGCE.

Profile: Bath Spa University

BATH SPA UNIVERSITY

Initial teacher education at Bath Spa University

Bath Spa University has a long tradition of initial teacher education (ITE), dating back over 60 years. Created as Bath Teacher Training College in 1947, the University is now the largest provider of ITE in the South West.

ITE programmes

The PGCE programme has been planned and developed in partnership with schools and educational settings to provide high-calibre new teachers to work in the twenty-first-century education system. We offer PGCE programmes in primary and early years (3–7 age phase; 5–11 age phase; 7–11 age phase) and secondary (11–16 age phase) in a range of subjects, including art and design, computer science, design and technology, English, maths, modern languages, music, PE, RE, biology, chemistry, physics and physics with maths.

In addition, we offer the following.

- School Direct: a new one-year school-based training route for graduates. You form part of a school team from day one and there is an expectation that you will be employed at the school on completion.

- Teach First: Bath Spa University works in partnership with education charity Teach First and the University of Bristol to train and support people with leadership potential to become inspirational teachers in schools in low-income areas in Bristol, Gloucester and Swindon. Bath Spa University leads on educating primary teachers on this two-year programme.

- Troops to Teachers: funded by the Department for Education, this programme aims to support a smooth transition into the civilian workforce for those service members who are exiting their military careers and considering becoming teachers.

Our philosophy

The ITE programme is underpinned by four key principles, which we believe are central to the process of becoming an effective teacher:

1. effective learning takes place when knowledge is shared and contested with a wide range of learning partners

2. professional discourse is robust and challenging

3. research is used to investigate and challenge current practice and shape new ideas

4. thinking skills are applied creatively and with purpose.

Bath Spa students will be expected to challenge their own thinking about the sort of teacher they are becoming, and how they will teach.

Highly rated by Ofsted

Bath Spa University has received a resounding endorsement for its teacher education programmes from the quality regulator Ofsted, achieving Grade 1, "Outstanding", across both primary and early years and secondary training. This confirms the University's status as not only the best teacher training university in the South West, but among the very best in the country.

Visit us

Bath Spa University has regular PGCE events for those wanting to find out more about becoming a teacher, and further information about these, and the PGCE programmes on offer, can be found on our website.

www.bathspa.ac.uk/teachingemail: teaching@bathspa.ac.uk

Telephone: 01225 875 624

Case study

Aaron Woodhouse

Aaron enrolled on our PGCE Programme in Secondary Mathematics. Here he tells us about his experience.

Q. What job did you do prior to enrolling on the PGCE programme?

I was teaching English as a foreign language in different parts of China for more than three years. I spent most of that time in a huge middle school in Shanghai, working with year 7 and 8 pupils who had varying English ability.

Q. Did you have the relevant qualifications to allow you to enrol, or did you need to top-up on any particular prerequisites?

My economics with accountancy degree didn't contain enough maths, and I hadn't been able to prove my mathematical ability with my previous jobs either. I therefore did Bath Spa University's six-month mathematics enhancement course (MEC). It was an intense six months, but it prepared me well for the PGCE.

Q. What prompted your decision to train to be a teacher?

I have always wanted to be a teacher and I had worked with children before. For example, I volunteered to help year 6 with their reading at a local school when I was studying for my undergraduate degree, and I also worked in a summer camp for four months in the USA. Having this experience of working with different age groups has helped me decide that I prefer working with secondary age pupils.

Q. What did you particularly like about the PGCE programme at Bath Spa?

I chose to do my PGCE at Bath Spa University because it has a proven track record of teacher training and the MEC I had taken there was extremely well run. I particularly liked the support and help given by tutors at university and mentors at both placement schools. I felt as though they were really there to help me and make sure I achieved my best.

Q. What preparation did you do before the programme?

I feel that the MEC prepared me really well for the PGCE. It showed me what to expect, and the high level of motivation, dedication and organisation needed to be successful on the PGCE.

Q. Describe the skills you learned from the PGCE programme.

The programme has given me the skills required to have a successful NQT year and teaching career. Not to mention that teaching is a continual learning curve. When starting my first teaching placement, I was surprised at the amount of time I would spend planning and preparing lessons. In the beginning, it takes a lot of time to prepare good lessons.

Q. What do you think makes a good teacher?

You need to be passionate about the subject and about working with young people. You should also be highly organised and motivated.

Q. What advice do you have for others wanting to take a teacher training programme?

If you've not already got some experience of working with young people then it's important to get some. And if that doesn't put you off, then go for it!

Keither Parker is the Head of Programme for Secondary Education at York St John University. Here, she describes the course she manages:

"Before our PGCE trainees begin, they are given an individualised programme to ensure they are fully prepared for the start of the course. So, for example, they undertake additional school experience, SKE and investigate current

affairs in education etc. This is considered essential to ensure they progress effectively.

"Trainees on the secondary programme are required to undertake 120 days on school placement and 60 days in university, as per the government requirements for the PGCE.

"The programme has been developed in partnership with our local schools to support effective integration of theory and practice, and our partnership schools are also involved in the recruitment of our PGCE trainees as well as their assessment.

"While in university, we endeavour to emulate a professional working environment and working day, so the trainees are expected to be in sessions from 9a.m. until 4p.m. every day of the week. Each day in university will be based either on either subject studies (such as English or history) or professional studies (where they look at whole-school issues such as planning, assessment or behaviour management).

"While trainees generally finish sessions by 4p.m., they are then expected to prepare for other sessions and will be reading and studying in relation to their assignments. Trainees on the PGCE programme often find this quite challenging and intense – particularly if they have joined us straight from an undergraduate programme, where they are used to being in lectures for only a small part of the week!

"Sessions in university include formal lectures and direct input from tutors, as well as active and enquiry-based learning activities and workshops where the trainees will input more themselves. We try to make the sessions as interactive as possible and model the teaching and learning strategies they will need to develop for their own professional practice.

"Assignments include essays, workshop presentations, a research project and a portfolio. Two assignments are at master's level and make up half of the 120 credits of the programme (required to achieve the PGCE).

"All trainees have an academic tutor who will meet them at least three times a year – they all have an individual action plan to support personalised learning and target-setting. Given the size of the cohort, the programme team will see trainees daily, so in addition to the formal academic tutor meetings, there is plenty of individual support.

"Trainees begin the programme with a short primary placement of one to two weeks, where they focus on issues related to progression and transition in their subject area. This also gives them the opportunity to focus on how children learn to read and other literacy issues.

"Then they are based in university for a few weeks before their first placement at a secondary school. Before this placement they have an opportunity to meet their subject mentor who will be supporting them in school. They will have five days (two days in one week and three in the next) prior to the placement to get to know the school, staff, pupils, policies and procedures and so on to ensure they make a positive start. At the end of the first placement, they return to university for a week before the Christmas break to do a placement debrief and set targets for the next term.

"In January, they start with a reading week to focus on assignments and then return to university for the second 'university block'. This is an important time to reflect on their own teaching practice in relation to the theory and help them integrate the two. During this time, they also have an 'enrichment' experience in an inner-city school to focus on diversity-related matters, such as children learning in schools with English as an additional language.

"In both of our secondary-school placements, trainees are supported with a subject mentor, a professional mentor (often a member of the school leadership team) and by a member of our PGCE programme team. We act as link tutors and visit the trainee at least twice on each placement to discuss their progress with them and their mentors. We also undertake *shared lesson appraisals with school mentors for quality assurance purposes.*

"The final part of the course is a lengthy final teaching placement that runs for 15 weeks from around the end or February or early March until the end of June. Following this, there is an 'enrichment' week in university with an opportunity to further develop an area of subject knowledge that trainees present at a final showcase event. This provides another opportunity to share effective practice and supports transition for the induction year. All members of the secondary school partnership are invited to this event, which also marks the end of the PGCE year. "

Many trainees comment on the steep learning curve of a PGCE route, so, however much support university tutors and school mentors provide, you will need to be ready for this.

Kirsty Anderson Dawes describes her experience doing a PGCE in Secondary Geography:

"Good organisation is key to success on the PGCE, as in teaching. The workload of the PGCE is high, and therefore being well organised is essential in ensuring that new teachers minimise stress on themselves. It's also worth bearing in mind that adjusting to a position of authority and responsibility can be difficult in the first term.

"The 'School Experience' part of the course lasts from the beginning of October until the beginning of December. Throughout this time, we are in school four days per week and return to university for one day a week. The time spent at university often helps to share experiences and reflect on them.

"We spend two weeks before Christmas back at university, where we complete a master's-level assignment and really begin to evaluate our experiences and set targets to meet in

the upcoming term. After Christmas, we have another week at university before going to our new Teaching Practice school, where we spend 14 weeks.

"Perseverance and patience are very important – not only in terms of teaching young people, but also in terms of your own development. It is very easy to get disheartened, as the PGCE is an intense rollercoaster of a year. It is very helpful if you have the ability to be reflective too, as we are required to keep a reflective journal for the duration of the course.

"A PGCE gives you the opportunity to study for master's credits alongside teacher training, so it suits students who are confident in academic study.

"The time at university helps to reinforce what happens at school and helps you make sense of it. It is quite difficult being both a student (at master's level) and a teacher. They both require very different skill sets and ask you to think in very different ways. This can be challenging.

"You get placed in several schools and therefore get an insight into different approaches and practices within education. I think this will be a positive experience that I can reflect on in job interviews, but being placed in several schools means that you only just begin to feel a part of the team and then change schools again. You live a slightly nomadic lifestyle for the PGCE year!"

Primary PGCEs are structured similarly in terms of the balance of school and university experience, but with much less emphasis on the single or dual subject knowledge that characterises secondary PGCEs. Primary PGCEs will spend more time on the core curriculum areas of English, maths and science and the foundation subjects of the primary National Curriculum.

Rachael Holmes is currently doing a primary PGCE at the University of Hull, and she describes her experiences so far:

"Being university-based, the PGCE was a more familiar route to me, and having some theoretical input from the university before going on placement was a good thing. I did not have enough experience to do the school-based route and I looked at Teach First, but I really did not want to go on the summer school or risk being put in a challenging school miles away from home.

"The course is 10 months in total, starting at the beginning of September and finishing in late June. The first teaching placement is four weeks long, the second is five weeks just after Christmas, and the third is eight weeks in the summer. The rest of the time is spent in university.

"University days are 9.15a.m. to 4.05p.m. with an hour for lunch. Core subjects are taught every week, as well as four hours of professional studies lectures and two-hour professional studies tutorials. The core subjects (English, mathematics and science) are taught on a three-week rolling rota to ensure that we have five or six three-hour sessions on each subject area. These are all taught by former primary school heads and teachers, as well as some current teaching staff from local schools. We have many half-days and additional days in school, especially in the lead-up to a teaching placement. I personally have visited seven different schools while at university.

"The only exams are the mandatory skills tests for maths and English, which we have to fit in around any free time. Assignments have consisted of four essays (three short essays and one extended, research-based essay), with the expectation of self-study on top of that. There are 17 smaller assignments based on observations or placement based assignments. These form our professional portfolio. We also have a teaching and professional development portfolio that demonstrates we have met the Teachers' Standards.

"Teaching expectations are limited on the first teaching placement (TP1) to about 25% of the time in class, but TP2 builds up to 60%–65% and 70%–75% on TP3. With each teaching placement, we have a different tutor, but we have the same professional studies tutor all year. We see our professional studies tutor every week while at university.

"Placement tutors visit us in school to check we are settling in, and then on TP1 they do one observation, two observations on TP2, and on TP3, three observations. Our school mentors are expected to have meetings with us regularly while on placement and do observations, as are our class teachers. I have felt really supported throughout my course and placements, and have only felt uncomfortable with one tutor.

"The university uses eBridge as its virtual learning environment (VLE), but it is not particularly easy or user-friendly. However, there is a forum for support, and tutors are really good at replying to queries quickly. Before the start of our course, a student set up a Facebook group that has about 75% of the course signed up, and has proved a good support for spreading ideas and help.

"Support on placements can be variable, though. Obviously experiences vary, but I have been very lucky and had some really great support, particularly in TP2 and so far in TP3 as well. This seems really welcoming, and I actually have an induction/welcome booklet to help me settle in and get to know the routines. I'm being treated like a member of staff from the start. Some TPs haven't been as well organised, but by the time you get to the last one you have a better idea of the information you need.

"I have had a lot of support, frequent meetings with and positivity from tutors. The university really does try to cover all bases and listen to students but then with tuition fees being around £9,000 for the year, we as a cohort have had high expectations with regard to getting value for money. It's also greatly increased my student debt.

"I have enjoyed the PGCE because I enjoy the academic side of teaching. You get experience in different schools with different tutors and different school mentors and teachers –

so you get a lot of support and advice from lots of different people, not just a limited few. I like the chance to share and discuss ideas with other students, former teachers and head teachers on a regular basis, and the general opportunities for reflection.

"I think PGCEs are really good if your confidence is not great at the beginning — I have really developed a lot in a very short space of time, and it's only a 10-month course, not a full year, so it does feel like a very short time to develop the skills needed to teach!"

7

School-based postgraduate SCITT route

If you are the kind of person who already has a considerable amount of relevant or associated experience – such as training, coaching or junior management – and has acquired a number of relevant skills – such as the ability to organise people, time and resources – and you are confident about your ability to get stuck in with the demands of a practical course, then you should consider the School-Centred Initial Teacher Training (SCITT) route.

The SCITT route is a model that is largely school-based and delivered by experienced teachers from a training base, or "lead school", where you will work with other trainees on professional and general aspects of becoming a qualified teacher, and then do long-term placements under the wing of a wider team of experienced teachers. They provide training and mentoring within a consortium of partner schools in the area or the region.

You will find SCITT providers that offer training across the statutory schooling phases – early years, primary and secondary – although many, if not most, will deal with only one or two. While all are self-accrediting providers of QTS, others are also partner of a local university and will offer a PGCE as part of the course.

The PGCE will be accredited by the university and will usually include credits towards an MA, and, in the view of one SCITT manager, this route in to teaching "offers bright candidates the highest level of award currently available with QTS".

Choosing a SCITT provider will usually find you in a relatively small group of trainees, around 20–40 people, most of whom will have had careers elsewhere, sometimes in other professions such as nursing, law or accountancy, though some will have worked in education as teaching assistants or in social work in a variety of roles. The demographic profile of those taking the SCITT route is usually quite mixed and interesting, and there is often a co-operative and collaborative feel about them – the groups are usually small enough for people to get to know and bond well with each other. This camaraderie is often fuelled by a shared sense of vulnerability – having moved out of the comfort zone of one's familiar work environment, people find ways of being supportive and mutually affirming.

Applying to SCITT courses

For a full range of SCITT teacher-training courses in England, you can visit the Graduate Teacher Training Registry at www.gttr.ac.uk. You can filter ITT providers on the basis of geographical area and subject.

As with all postgraduate routes, in order to apply to train as a teacher through the SCITT route you must have a UK undergraduate degree or a recognised equivalent qualification, GCSE grade C or above in English and mathematics and, if you are applying to teach primary or at Key Stage 2–3 (7–14 years old), you must also have a science subject at grade C or above.

Be aware that SCITT courses are limited in number and often fill up quite early in the application cycle, so you should be thinking of making your application in the autumn of the year before you want to start your training. Application through GTTR opens in mid-October, so you should be thinking of making your application to your chosen provider as soon as possible after that.

While SCITT consortia are widely available around England, there are currently none in Wales, Scotland or Northern Ireland, but some in England may use certain schools in Wales to deliver their training.

Also, note that the Scottish education system does not automatically recognise the English school- or employment-based routes to QTS. So if you wanted to move to Scotland to teach after qualifying via this route, you may need to do a top-up qualification such as a PGDE in order to get QTS in Scotland. For more information, go to the General Teaching Council for Scotland website (www.gtcs. org.uk) and click on the "Qualified Outside of Scotland".

What to expect on an SCITT course

You will spend somewhere between one-quarter and one-third of your time at the lead-school base, or at university doing general, professional or academic sessions on the taught part of the course, although secondary SCITT students will generally spend more time in school than their primary counterparts.

Some consortia will have a small group of partner schools, perhaps five to ten within a town or borough, while others will have as many as 20–25 in the consortium and might be spread over quite a large geographical area such as a rural county. These providers have enabled many people to train who wouldn't have otherwise had access to teacher training, so they have often attracted those living in relatively remote or rural areas.

You will spend about two-thirds to three-quarters of your time (about 16–18 weeks) at your main placement school, and the teachers in those partner placement schools act as mentors to organise and monitor your training.

You will feel pretty much part of your main placement school right from the beginning – indeed, many trainees following this route comment that they "were treated like and even referred to as teachers from day one". Consequently, you will have plenty of opportunity to be involved in a wide range of school activities, such as staff meetings, parents' evenings, development days, school concerts, plays, clubs and sports days.

Additionally, you will also have the opportunity of a short placement in a second school for between four and six weeks, with other regular day visits to different schools to see exceptionally good general or special needs practice, or to get some observational experience of a different phase.

Veronica Towers manages the Wandsworth Primary Schools' Consortium. Here she describes the structure and content of her course:

"We currently have 30 trainees on our course. It has 18 weeks taught and three weeks directed study, with a minimum of 19 weeks on placement plus half-day visits and workshops with pupils adding up to approximately another full week. This will increase to 24 weeks from 2013.

"Our trainees are placed in a minimum of two schools, including a paired placement in an alternate Key Stage for six weeks – so for example, if they are training mainly for Key Stage 2, they will also have at least six weeks' placement in Key Stage 1. Visits to schools, especially for early years trainees, add up to about another full week in school. Part of the selection process involves candidates working for half a day in one of the consortium schools.

"We are very closely connected to our partner consortium schools, and head teachers help to interview all candidates and shortlist applications. There are no exams but there are essays: four of them with two at master's level, including an area of research interest. Our assessment methods, therefore, are mainly down to the assessments of the school-based mentor and our own tutor supervision. During the placement, there are also quality assurance visits from internal and external examiners and sometimes Ofsted, but we pride ourselves on very strong individual support – both pastoral and academic.

"In my view, the SCITT route combines the best of university and school as the small size of the cohort in effect models a class of pupils working with their teacher or tutor.

"Most years, all but one or two trainees are career-changers, many coming from backgrounds in law, acting, sales, advertising and teaching assistant roles. They bring transferable skills and are keenly motivated to be the best that they can.

"The most successful trainees are those who enjoy working collaboratively and are generous in giving time and support to one another. Some personalities prefer to be focused on the daily work of teaching without significant time given to reflection about pedagogy or theories about education, but in my view, the SCITT–PGCE combination offers bright candidates the highest level of award currently available with QTS. "

The structure of the course is broadly the same for secondary trainees as it is for primary, although subject specialism requirements mean that secondary trainees spend a little longer in schools. Here Bryn Harrison, the manager of a SCITT course based at a large Catholic secondary school in Swindon, describes the contrasting model he runs there:

"We currently have 26 trainees covering a wide variety of subject areas for teaching at 11–16. It's a full-time course of 36 weeks. The central training at the school base consists of professional studies, covering whole-school issues, and this lasts for 10 weeks overall. Then there's the subject-specific training, which is co-ordinated by a subject leader at the lead school and lasts for 26 weeks overall.

"There are three school placements in two different schools. We offer QTS and a PGCE at honours or master's level – validated by the University of Bath – and the master's-level work gains credits towards a master's degree if the trainees want it. There are three assignments during the course: a subject-specific task, a subject-specific assignment and a general educational study, which is a piece of action research. Each school placement is assessed in relation to the Teachers' Standards, and the final placement assessment is summative and determines the award of QTS. The trainees also compile an e-portfolio to demonstrate evidence of meeting the standards.

"In my view, the main advantage of the SCITT route is the time spent in school developing teaching competencies, supported by a coherent central training programme. This allows time for reflection and the development of a theoretical model for teaching.

"Our SCITT is in its 10th year in 2013, and many of our mentors are former SCITT trainees — which means they understand the course structure, content and the demands made on trainees such as assignments and so on.

"The small size of the cohorts means the course can easily be tailored to meet individual needs, and targeted personalised support can be offered when trainees find certain things challenging. The inclusion of the PGCE qualification also adds academic rigour and puts the classroom practice into a wider context. There is close involvement with the partner schools and this enables a wide range of people to review and evaluate all aspects of the course so that constant improvements can be made. "

If you choose a SCITT consortium that runs its course with a university to include a PGCE, and most people do, you will almost certainly be required to attend some lectures at the university as part of your course. Most trainees soon realise that while the academic side of training imposes additional demands (such as study and essay writing) on skills that may have become a little rusty, it is an important part of becoming a fully qualified practitioner in a profession such as teaching.

If you believe that teaching is a profession, you will readily accept that studying and understanding educational theory is essential to educational practice. Indeed, solid grounding in theory is often what teachers fall back on when the going gets tough and solely pragmatic approaches start to fail. Teaching is not a bag of tricks that relies on coming up with creative ideas every Sunday evening before you start your week in the classroom. It relies on reflection and analysis of what is going on in front of you. You'll be able to do that so much more effectively if you have some knowledge and understanding of theories of learning. After all, would we expect a doctor or a lawyer to be fully qualified if they had only learned their skills on the job?

So if you do decide that the school-based training route is for you, don't let the reason be that academic theory is not important. It is — and what's more, the more seriously you take the academic and theoretical side of your training, the better practitioner you will be in the long run.

Leading education and social research
Institute of Education
University of London

Class.
Leader.

Rated outstanding by Ofsted, train to teach at primary, secondary or post-compulsory level.

Inspiring Ongoing Excellence

Learn more: ioe.ac.uk/ITT
enquiries@ioe.ac.uk
or call +44 (0)20 7612 6100

Where do the inspirational get their inspiration?

BATH SPA UNIVERSITY

DIFFERENT THINKING

Teacher Education – learn to inspire.

Rated Outstanding (Grade 1) by Ofsted, our Teacher Education PGCE programmes cover Primary and Early Years, and Secondary Education.

Working closely with schools and other key partners, we offer inspiring programmes to support the education of new teachers, children, young people and their communities.

If you're feeling inspired, discover more online or visit us at one of our events.

bathspa.ac.uk/teaching

Ofsted
Outstanding
2010 | 2011

University of Hertfordshire — UH — School of **Education**

Your knowledge

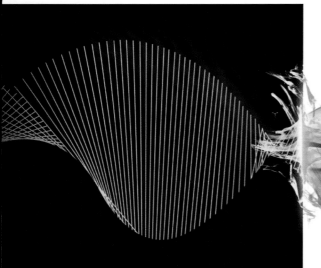

will ignite imaginations

Teaching is a highly demanding but incredibly rewarding career. Train to teach at Herts – one of the leading regional providers of Initial Teacher Education – and we will equip you with the knowledge, confidence and practical skills you need to make a real impact in the world of education.

Become more.

Find out about our range of courses at:
go.herts.ac.uk/education_w

At the heart of world thinking

Initial Teacher Education

At King's we offer the PGCE either led by the university or in partnership with a school through School Direct. We also offer School Direct Salaried (Qualified Teacher Status (QTS) only).

Why train to be a Teacher at King's?

- You will be challenged to take a critical view of policies and practice.

- You will work with others and discuss current issues in teaching.

- You will work with tutors who are actively engaged in research in their subject and about teaching.

- We are located in the heart of London.

- We were rated as Outstanding by Ofsted.

Subject specialisms available in:

Biology Chemistry Classics Computer Science English IT and Computer Science Mathematics Modern Foreign Languages Physics Physics with Mathematics Religious Education

www.kcl.ac.uk/pgce

The Cambridge Partnership

Initial Teacher Training

So you want to be a teacher......

Have you got what it takes?

- ✓ Have you got a degree?

- ✓ Have you got English and Mathematics GCSE at grade C or above?

- ✓ Are you determined, enthusiastic, caring, inspiring, motivating?

- ✓ Do you have passion for your subject that you want to share?

So what's stopping you?

Tel **01487 833707** or email

info@thecambridgepartnership.co.uk

The Cambridge Partnership, The Tony Robinson Centre,
Sawtry Community College,
Fen Lane, Sawtry, PE28 5TQ

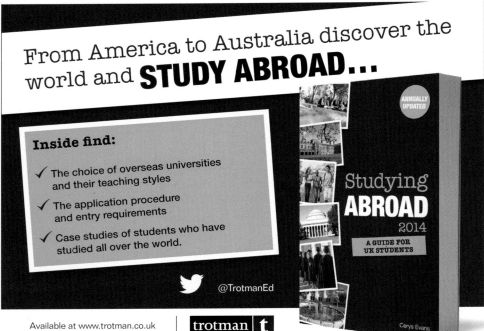

Here's the view of Louise Foster who trained via a primary SCITT route in Nottingham a few years ago:

"I have always been an organised person with good time-management skills, and I thought that these would lend themselves well to teaching. I am also patient and hard working. I knew from my previous experiences that I would perform best in a SCITT, where I could get to know the staff and children really well and become a part of the team, rather than do a PGCE where I would be in multiple short placements. I was always quite shy, and it took me a while to settle into places and feel at ease. Also, I was used to working in schools and I liked the feeling of being a part of the team and getting to know one class really well.

"I was based in one school with my mentor's class for the majority of the year, full-time. I had three teaching-placement blocks during the year, apart from my base class, a two-week placement in a different school and a three-week placement in another class at the base school. The whole trainee group also attended two, five-day training sessions at Nottingham University: one in August before the course started, and the other during the Easter holidays. We had five assignments to do throughout the year, in our own time. Four were marked by the school mentor, and the dissertation was marked by the university. We also had weekly reading and study tasks.

"We also attended approximately one training day per half term at another school – usually, these were subject-based, in order to see good practice. The school mentor did all the observations and marked assessments, and we were expected to teach lessons from our first week at the school. Gradually, this was increased, so we were full=time teachers by the last half term.

"On the SCITT route, you certainly get to know what working as a full-time teacher is like from day one, so this is a great route if you have already had experience of working in schools.

"What you have to remember, though, is that you need to have good organisational and time-management skills, as you are doing the work of a full-time teacher as well as assignments and study weeks. Also, if there is a personality clash between the trainee and the school mentor, you are stuck there for a year and it could affect your achievements.

"But the SCITT route helps you to learn all of the extra parts of the job that you may not experience on short placements. For example, I was involved in parents' evenings, staff meetings and writing reports. It provided me with lots of regular feedback so I could continually improve my teaching. I had a range of colleagues available to ask for advice and support and the whole experience gave me a lot of confidence that I could do the job."

Laura Harris, who is currently doing her primary SCITT course in the West Country, offers a complementary view. In her account, the knowledge that comes with experience and maturity clearly informed her decision to choose this route.

"Coming to teaching in my mid-30s meant that I had experience of several roles prior to commencing the course. Having children myself, and having both volunteered and worked in pre-school, primary, secondary and college environments, I always knew I wanted to work with children.

"I think I am an empathetic, thoughtful and reflective person, so my earlier roles in schools meant I was able to build a good rapport with children based on trust and mutual respect. Having experience of a wide variety of learning environments and age groups, I knew that secondary school was the best fit for me personally.

"I spoke to many of the trainee teachers who came through the school and heard lots of very favourable things about SCITT courses. I was told that as the SCITT courses had fewer trainees than other university-based courses, the students were able to build good personal relationships with other trainees, and this provides invaluable support.

"Finally, because I have children settled in local schools, I would have been unable to pursue courses that required large amounts of travelling due to childcare commitments. As such, the course was an excellent match for me, both personally and practically.

"It's organised around three placements (the first and third in the same school to allow progression to be tracked; the second placement is in a contrasting school).

In the first half of term one, there are three weeks of central training (this includes an introduction to the course and two days at the base school). This is followed by four weeks in your main placement school (with one day a week at central training at the SCITT base school). In the second half of that term, we have five weeks at the main placement school (with one day a week at central training), followed by a two-week block at central training (including two days visiting our second placement school). In the first half of the next term, we have a full five weeks at the second placement school.

"In half-term four, we have one full week at our second placement school, followed by one week in central training, then return to our main placement school (with one day a week at central training) for the remaining three weeks. In half-term five we have one week in central training followed by six full weeks at our main placement school. In the last half term, we have four full weeks at our main placement school, followed by four days in central training to conclude the course.

"There are two main written assignments: one is a 5,000-word subject-specific assignment, and the other is a 5,000-word educational study. We each have a mentor and professional tutor in both school placements, and we have tutorial sessions each term with a member of the course team. We also have a subject mentor who we meet with during our central training days.

"In my view, the SCITT route allows for smaller number of trainees leading to more individualised support, and as it is school-based, there is a greater number of in-school days with strong links to local schools — so I think it is an excellent route into teaching."

8

School-based postgraduate School Direct route

The School Direct training programme is an entirely new school-based route to qualify as a teacher, introduced by the government in England in 2012. It is a one-year employment-based training course, and although it is a new training route into teaching, it is most similar in terms of its structure and content to the Graduate Teacher Programme (GTP) that it replaced. The emphasis is on acquiring teaching skills, so this route will suit those with a strong background in the subject they want to teach and who are confident of their ability to cope with the stresses and strains of the often intense practical demands that teacher training can impose.

The trainees who will thrive in this form of training are those with considerable experience of work, particularly previous management or professional responsibilities. Parents who have had direct and daily experience of bringing up small children in a family, and who have acquired many of the skills in managing and engaging with young children, may be particularly suited to training as nursery or primary teachers through this route.

One of the main attractions of this route is that, while it does not guarantee a job at the end of the training, there is a clear expectation that you will employed by the school or the group of schools where you have been based for the training period. Schools themselves, rather than universities, are directly involved in the selection of their trainees via this route, and many School Direct training providers will have had substantial experience in training teachers prior to the scheme, perhaps having run a GTP scheme or been designated as a training school. Depending on which School Direct provider you apply to, you may have the opportunity to acquire a PGCE (or similar) as part of the training, if the provider has established an arrangement with a local university as part of the route to qualification.

As with all postgraduate routes, in order to apply to train as a teacher through the School Direct programme you must have a UK undergraduate degree or a recognised equivalent qualification, GCSE grade C or above in English and mathematics and, if you are applying to teach primary or at Key Stage 2–3 (7–14-year-olds), you must also have a science subject at grade C or above.

The School Direct training programme offers two routes:

1. **the salaried route:** where you will be employed by a school and have a salary for the duration of the training; or

2. **the student route:** where you will be attached to a school and may be eligible for a bursary but will pay student fees.

The salaried route

If you apply for School Direct's salaried route, you will need to show you have at least three years' relevant work experience. This is an essential requirement, but it need not necessarily be experience working with children in schools. Relevant positions could include those where you might have been responsible for managing, training or coaching adults, or in commerce or industry with responsibility for apprentices or trainees, or where you were planning and delivering courses or projects in organised and methodical ways.

As these places essentially provide a salaried position with a strong expectation of a permanent job at the end of it, they are in much greater demand – so the number of these places available is strictly limited.

Profile: King's College London

Training to become a teacher at the Department of Education and Professional Studies, King's College London

The Department of Education and Professional Studies at King's has a worldwide reputation for its quality of research, curriculum development, teaching and teacher training. Rated one of the country's top education departments for research in the last Research Assessment Exercise (RAE), our strong, dynamic research culture informs all our teaching.

King's College London

King's College London is one of the top 30 universities in the world (2012–13 QS international world rankings) and was voted "Best University for Graduate Employment 2012–13" by the *Sunday Times*. The Department of Education and Professional Studies is based in the heart of London at the College's Waterloo Campus, an excellent location close to the South Bank.

The Department of Education and Professional Studies

The Department of Education and Professional Studies has an international reputation for the quality of its research, curriculum development, teaching and teacher training. We were rated one of the country's top education departments for research in the last RAE, and our strong and dynamic research culture permeates our teaching.

Initial teacher education

At King's College London we offer the PGCE either led by the university or in partnership with a school through School Direct. We also offer School Direct salaried leading to QTS. We are an "Outstanding" provider.

The King's PGCE is an ITT programme leading to QTS for teaching in secondary schools (ages 11–18). We work in close partnership with schools in designing, delivering and assessing our programme, and applicants have the opportunity to work with tutors who are actively engaged in research and are encouraged to take a critical view of policies and practice.

School Direct is a new mode of ITT in which schools work closely with college tutors to ensure that trainees are well prepared to work in schools. The aim is for trainees to take up teaching posts in the school or consortium of schools in which they train, once they have qualified.

Case study

Rebecca Purser

Rebecca took a PGCE Mathematics in 2009–10 following her undergraduate maths degree. She really enjoyed the experience of being thrown in at the deep end, as she relates below.

I had always thought I would go into teaching later on in life, but as soon as I started the PGCE at King's I knew I had made the right choice. I thought I knew a lot about teaching, but soon realised that I knew very little. The tutors at King's really made us think in those first few weeks about understanding the systems and structures in school, but more importantly about understanding the mathematics and being able to help students in our classes really comprehend what they were doing.

It was great to get into a school really quickly and get stuck in. You can get so much from observing the teachers and students in schools and start to think about what sort of teacher you will be. The main thing I wanted to do was start teaching, though, and as daunting as it seemed, it was good to get it out of the way and develop more confidence. The schools have well-trained mentors on hand for any questions you may have and generally the culture in schools is to support and encourage new staff and professional development.

The college days were good to share stories with fellow PGCE students and offer support and advice to each other. The sessions were really thought-provoking and left you full of ideas for your next week in schools. I was a bit nervous about the written assignments, as, coming straight from doing a maths degree, my experience of written work was fairly limited. I chose topics for the two assignments that I was really interested in, and with some guidance and feedback from the King's tutors I was able to be a lot more successful at these than I thought.

I got very caught up with the research and assignments and soon had the bug to carry on, so I was first in line to sign up to the MA Mathematics Education course. It was so rewarding doing this, and has made me really reflect on the daily business of being a teacher, meaning that I have been able to be more critical of some practices but also keep the passion and creativity in my teaching.

I am now just finishing my third year of teaching and have been a PGCE mentor for two of those years. I also have the responsibility of being second in charge in the maths department, and I am working with senior staff implementing strategies to give students the best learning experience. My interest in research has continued; I am still in touch with my King's tutors and next year I'm planning to work with them on a statistics teaching project, which will feed information back to senior staff in my school. I don't know what the future holds; I never thought I would be doing all the things I am doing so soon. That's the beauty of teaching, every day is different and there are so many varied opportunities out there.

The tuition fee route

If you apply to School Direct's tuition fee route, the course structure and content is exactly the same. Indeed, you will be training and teaching in schools alongside your colleagues on the salaried route. However, you will be required to pay student fees for the course (this could be up to £9,000 a year, although many School Direct providers charge substantially less). There are bursaries available to pay this and to help with your living costs; and, depending on your phase and subject, you stand a good chance of being awarded one. For example, tax-free bursaries of up to £20,000 are available for those with good science, mathematics and some MFL degrees, for both secondary and primary trainees. Additionally, some professional bodies for the maths and sciences are also offering scholarships of up to £20,000 to support their graduates going into teaching.

Darren Barton is Director of the Wessex Schools Training Programme, and runs a School Direct training programme from Poole in Dorset:

> "We can get around 100–150 applicants a year although we only have about 15 secondary places to offer – so the competition is stiff. While the trainees are employed in our partner schools either here in Poole or across Dorset, our course includes four weeks studying professional themes and weekly mentor meetings. Trainees also have around 15 bespoke subject tutorials over the length of the course to improve their subject knowledge, and two 4,000-word assignments to complete that focus on methods of assessment and personal, learning and thinking skills. The trainees get a lot of additional mentor support, feedback from regular observations, and reviews of their files where they collect evidence that they are addressing the Teachers' Standards.
>
> "We think the mentor support is a great strength of the scheme because both the mentor and the trainee are based in the same school and we think this leads to trainees being very prepared for their NQT year. Trainees literally hit the ground running. It is harder work than a PGCE, but if you are on the salaried route at least you get paid for it!"

As Darren describes, most providers of the School Direct scheme will have small groups of trainees. That may be a positive feature for you. On the other hand, you are likely to have only a very small cohort of colleagues training in the same subject. You may even be the only one if you are training to be an RE, citizenship, business studies or psychology teacher. If you are the kind of person who likes to bounce ideas off other students and establish a wider network of subject support through your peers then this might be an issue (compared for example, with a large cohort of history or English trainees on a university-based PGCE).

This leads on to another issue that might affect your choice of School Direct provider. Because the schools themselves employ the trainees and manage the process of selection, they are very close to the employment needs and demands of the partner schools involved. It may be that on a given year, the particular School Direct provider near you is not offering any places for history, geography or other humanities trainees because none of the partner schools can foresee imminent vacancies arising. On the other hand, a local university offering a secondary PGCE course may have a number of places earmarked for training humanities trainees, irrespective of the immediate employment needs of local schools. If your chosen subject or phase happens not to be in the current peak of teacher demand, then finding a School Direct place, particularly a salaried one, may prove difficult.

Charlotte Hopperton trained via this route in 2012, and describes her experience:

> "In all honesty, it was mostly down to the financial side of things. I was in no position to pay university tuition fees and needed a salaried way of training. But what really sold the course to me was the level of responsibility and involvement with students.
>
> "I was employed by the school and it provided an educational mentor and subject mentor. Throughout the academic year, my timetable increased from 0% to 80% of a teacher's timetable. I was expected to attend about 20–25 university days, of which approximately 15 were compulsory and the rest optional. I had to complete various portfolio folders to demonstrate that I had obtained knowledge and certain skills, while providing

evidence for my final qualification. I also had a university mentor who would visit each term to assess my progress. For me the pros were:

- you experience a whole school year from start to end, which allows you to learn the highs and lows as well as the times of year that can be particularly difficult

- you're paid to teach – this is financially a far more viable position in light of the current economic climate

- being employed by the school, so you are made to feel as if you are a teacher from the word go, rather than being a trainee and therefore a student of sorts

- the work–life balance – I think you start establishing balanced routines earlier

- access to a wealth of knowledge – by being in a school, you can access both new and well–established teachers who can give you guidance on a range of techniques, styles and experiences

- you can build a better rapport with students, parents and staff by staying in the school, which means you aren't just "the PGCE student" but actually "the teacher"

- the practical application of teaching is a doddle! You learn to think on your feet and adapt lessons based on the feel of the classroom, rather than trying to simply apply a theory and then retrospectively altering it for the future.

- But the cons were:

- you can feel incredibly isolated if you are the only trainee in a school; if you befriend PGCEs or other students training there, don't be surprised that you find yourself a little lonely after they have gone!

- you feel like a rubbish trainee at times — you exhibit tenfold all the bad habits that you'll be told trainees shouldn't develop

- it is incredibly exhausting — nobody said teaching was easy, but it most certainly is a shock to the system when you have to attend all the same things that teachers do too

- theory is somewhat of a mystery to you — a bit of an abstraction — and that's not helpful being trained to specialise in one type of school or style of teaching; that can be a hindrance when it comes to job hunting.

"If you love a challenge then go for this route. Overall, I came into teaching with my eyes open, knowing what to expect from an academic year and being prepared to face students with my own experience.

"I was incredibly lucky to be placed in a very knowledgeable, supportive and caring school. There was an established network of people whom I could call on for support, and never once did I feel as if I was a burden. Overall, I cannot really fault the quality of teaching and support that I received."

Another trainee who took this route last year, Lubna, summed up her experience like this:

"The pros are, first, the salary! Then, by applying to a local provider, you get more say in choosing your school or schools. You also develop a relationship over time with your mentor that is so important to your success. I also think you are treated more like a proper teacher than a student teacher, as you're fully immersed in school life from day one of the academic year. You teach your own classes throughout the year and so build up great relationships with students and are therefore able to plan, teach and assess them so much better.

"The cons are that this method will only suit those with proper experience either in schools or in relevant work. I thought I had plenty of experience in school, but there was still a lot to learn about policies, procedures and professionalism. Sometimes changes in the circumstances of a department can greatly affect the level of support you get too. One girl I knew was acting as head of department while training due to her mentor being signed off sick.

"However, overall I thought this route prepared me absolutely brilliantly."

9

School-based postgraduate Teach First route

Teach First is a small but growing training provider that targets top graduates from top universities to train as teachers in areas of very challenging socio-economic circumstances. Although it is a charity, its aim is to develop people with leadership potential to become inspirational teachers in some of the UK's toughest schools. It's an idea based on a US model (Teach for America) that attracts talented and highly able graduates to try teaching before being tempted by employment and potentially greater riches in the corporate world.

Currently, Teach First recruits about 1,200–1,300 candidates a year, with more than half of those who complete the two-year programme continuing to stay in teaching. Obviously not all who start the training stay the full two years to complete it, and as is the case with other routes into teaching, retention rates drop off particularly after five years. Nevertheless, the competition is very intense for Teach First places, and it has a very good reputation with its partner universities and schools for setting high standards.

The training begins with six weeks of an intensive "Summer Institute", delivered with one of the six partner universities around the country. Accommodation, transport and food expenses are all provided.

Then, at the beginning of term, trainees are placed in one of their partner schools, all situated in areas of socio-economic deprivation. Once in school, trainees are given teaching responsibilities right from the beginning, with the support of school-based mentors and other mentors from Teach First. If all goes well, they will achieve a PGCE at the end of the first year.

What is highly distinctive about the Teach First programme is that it focuses right from the start on developing leadership skills, so alongside the school-based training of classroom skills and meeting the standards for QTS, there is a leadership development programme that includes coaching and mentoring, networking and internship opportunities.

At the end of the first year, trainees can use the credits gained as part of the PGCE to commit to an optional two-year master's degree.

It's probably fair to say that Teach First selects people who will be highly committed to their overall mission of tackling educational disadvantage, and who will be very enthusiastic, even zealous, about promoting that cause. Admirably, they try to sustain that commitment whether or not trainees decide to stay in teaching, and at the end of the programme graduates are inducted to become a Teach First Ambassador.

In the first year, Teach First trainees will be paid at least the basic salary for an unqualified teacher. This rises in year two to the basic salary for an NQT. However, it is not uncommon for Teach First trainees to earn more than this, in some cases quite a lot more depending on the region, the school, and any management responsibilities that the school feels ready to delegate and they themselves are happy to take on. It is not uncommon, for example, for trainees to have taken on departmental, year group or leadership responsibilities at quite an early stage.

Laura McInerney did the Teach First programme a few years ago:

> "I did my six weeks Summer Institute at Canterbury Christ Church University and was then placed in a school in east London. There are almost weekly observations throughout the first year until you achieve QTS, and once a term we had a study day without university tutors, but now people completing the programme also do university essays to achieve a PGCE.

"Induction for Teach Firsters is during the second year of the programme. There is still support from a Teach First learning development officer who will visit and observe practice, but your school also provides training sessions and observations from a school-based mentor.

"My induction was a little odd as I had to do the training and observations during both years of Teach First. This is quite common for those on the scheme, but it can be a little annoying if your school makes you sit through the same programme again. Thankfully, my school had me work with the NQT induction tutor in the second year and I helped to deliver several of the sessions. Doing so advanced my practice more quickly and helped give me greater confidence.

"All the support and mentoring I received through Teach First and my school were excellent. I think I was very lucky!"

Melissa Fearon became a modern languages teacher through this route, and her account reflects some of the passion and zeal common with many who have completed Teach First:

"Teach First made me want to become a teacher. I would not have entered teaching any other way. On a practical level, I could not have afforded to go into teaching had it not been for Teach First. Straight from university, I needed to be earning and working. Teach First gives you the advantage of being able to earn, gain hands-on teaching experience and study for free, and to work towards its fantastic mission — to address educational disadvantage."

She goes on to describe the structure and content of the programme:

"First, the Summer Institute is six weeks of intense training at university with mentors, teaching professionals and other Teach First participants. Then straight into school and your first year of teaching as an unqualified teacher — you'll have 80% of a full timetable, and when you're not teaching you are doing essays and coursework, working towards your PCGE. It is funded by Teach First, so there are no university fees, and we are paid an entry-level graduate salary, which increases in the second year.

"At the end of the first year you have a six-week summer project and the chance to work with a business sponsor (or whomever we chose). Teach First has hundreds of sponsors and businesses giving you the chance to do a six-week paid internship over this summer. Sponsors include Google, PriceWaterhouseCoopers, Clifford Chance, Save the Children and Accenture.

"Then the second year of teaching: teaching as an NQT with QTS! You have the opportunity to take on more responsibility within the school, be it a pastoral or a departmental role, and there's still support to develop your subject knowledge and leadership skills from mentors in school and from Teach First.

"There is also the option of taking a master's qualification if you want. It is part-time, running over two years (with the aim of finishing it one year after the programme ends). It has a small fee, but there are three master's degrees available: a master's in Leadership, a master's in Education, and a master's in Leadership in Education.

"Then there's the ambassador network. On completing the two-year programme you become a Teach First ambassador, continuing the programme's mission with initiatives such as Achieve Together and the Higher Education Access Programme for Schools (HEAPS). Whether you continue in education or go into business, you are expected to continue to help Teach First as an ambassador.

"This is an ideal course for anybody who believes they have the resilience, the ambition and the drive to jump in at the deep end. Teach First accepts graduates with no teaching experience, but its recruitment process follows that of other graduate schemes, where experience in roles of responsibility and emotional intelligence is imperative.

"However, some may find it a lot to handle at once: with just six weeks of training before you are expected to teach a class of 30 disadvantaged pupils, some may feel out of their depth, despite the wealth of support and expertise."

As Melissa says, Teach First will appeal to those who have bags of resilience and ambition, and perhaps the deeply rooted self-confidence that often comes with high-achieving graduates. But it is a scheme that, even though you will have excellent support and mentoring, puts you right in at the deep end in some of the country's toughest schools. It is also a scheme that asks you to commit to its mission whether or not you continue to stay in teaching – and that is a consideration which, while not unreasonable and certainly admirable, may not be something you are prepared to undertake.

What stands out about Teach First, though, is that if you are both able and ambitious, it will take those qualities and develop them in ways that other routes do not have the resources to support, such as the business sponsor internship scheme.

If you are a high-achieving, self-starting, ambitious, mature, strong, and irrepressible person who has natural leadership qualities, and who is passionate about addressing the greatest educational issue of our time, then training to become a teacher through Teach First may be for you.

PART 3
Your first year as a teacher

10

Getting your first teaching job

Most teachers, eager to secure a job and start work, will take the first position that is offered to them. Often, that turns out to be the school where they did their final teaching practice – which is usually a good fit for both school and trainee. Given the intense competition for jobs these days, it is understandable why as a new teacher you might leap on to the first offer and take it – but be careful. Choosing the right school might have far-reaching implications, not just for how happy and supported you feel in the first few years of your new career, but for what kind of teacher you go on to become. Finding and choosing a good school that fits your values and aspirations is therefore a very important decision.

Teachers' terms and conditions require them to give a long period of notice, at least half a term or about three months, which means that most jobs are advertised quite a long time in advance of starting. Most maintained (state) schools adhere to the three-term year currently co-ordinated by local authorities. However, some local variations are creeping in, with Academies and Free Schools varying term dates and of course, very late or early Easters (which are determined by the lunar calendar). Some national variations, such as the summer and autumn terms starting and ending earlier in Scotland and Northern Ireland, are more marked. By and large though, school teaching terms fall in to:

- autumn term: beginning of September to the end of December

- spring term: beginning of January to the middle or end of April

- summer term: middle or end of April to end of July.

However, teachers are bound by resignation deadline dates that are unchanging. These are:

- 31 October for resignation at the end of the autumn term (to finish on 31 December)

- 28 February for resignation at the end of the spring term (to finish on 30 April), and

- 31 May for resignation at the end of the summer term (to finish on 31 August).

The great bulk of annual vacancies are for appointments to begin at the beginning of the school year in September. There are two reasons for this – first, most teachers decide to move schools or retire from teaching at the end of the summer term. Secondly, most teacher trainees will graduate in summer (for a first appointment in September). Most people, then, will be searching for their first teaching job any time from early spring through to the end of the summer. However, some last-minute appointments are even made right at the end of August.

There are some exceptions to this, of course, if you train through a flexible route (such as a part-time PGCE, School Direct or a SCITT course) that allow for a staggered start and end to the training.

Whatever time of year you are applying, you need to pay close attention to two key issues:

1. finding good, plentiful and suitable sources of job vacancies

2. the "look and feel" of a school and whether you are the right fit for it.

Finding plentiful and suitable job sources

The competition for jobs these days is intense, and so you will need to make job searching a priority, particularly in the final six months of your course. Many trainees still get job offers from the school where they have done their final teaching practice and, of course, if you choose an employment-based route, you may have a job almost (although not definitely) guaranteed at the end of it. However, the vast majority of those training to be teachers will need to search and apply for an appointment.

These days, most people search for jobs on the internet, and you will quickly become acquainted with the top sites for teaching job searches such as:

- www.tes.co.uk/jobs

- www.jobs.guardian.co.uk/jobs/education

- www.eteach.com.

There are, of course, many more, and just googling "teaching jobs" with your area added will throw up dozens of sites run by agencies – these will host job adverts for both full-time and part-time permanent positions, as well as supply posts, which are usually short- or even very short-term temporary positions. You don't need to register yourself exclusively to any particular agency, so sign up with as many as possible, but make sure you refine and customise your search preferences so you are not wasting your time trawling through jobs that are not relevant to you.

Teaching agencies

Agencies are often small operations run by a few staff, specialising in providing teachers for local schools. As a result, they often know the local employment patterns of supply and demand quite well, especially if they have built up a reputation for providing good-quality supply teachers.

Other agencies are very large, and the sections dealing with teachers are a branch of a much larger offering to the commercial, technical or industrial sectors. While they may have less of a personalised, local feel about them, they usually have substantial resources to advertise and attract clients. Both kinds of agency have their merits and downsides. Sign up to all of them and get a feel for how well they deal with you as an individual and your particular needs.

It's debatable whether it's worth buying newspapers and publications for job hunting any more, but *The Times Education Supplement* (*TES*), the *Guardian* and even the *Independent* newspapers were at one time popular for this. Now search engines can customise and save your job search preferences very effectively by region, town and city, subject, phase and even school type. However, *The TES* and the *Guardian* still do publish special editions and supplements in newspaper format for NQTs seeking first appointments that also include tips for application and interview preparation. Additionally, they will also regularly host online Q&A sessions or discussion forums related to job hunting and advice for first appointments.

Choosing the right school

Most people finish their training course and take the first job that comes along. Often that's out of fear that they won't be offered something else, or because most of them have got very few reference points by which to judge a school. Perhaps the only yardstick they have are the schools they did their teaching practices in — and that may be as few as two.

It's a tough call to judge a school on a short visit. They are complex and organic communities, and the atmosphere can sometimes feel very different from one day to the next. As a relatively inexperienced new teacher, you may be impressionable. For example, you may see and hear things in one school that strike you as odd — such as the way children address adults, including teachers, by their first name being the norm. At another, you may find the buildings awkwardly and inconveniently arranged, with for instance some classrooms being in Portakabins situated well away from the main building. However, as a new teacher you are also likely to be robust, and you will get used to strange, new ways very quickly.

Don't be too swayed by the outward, physical impressions of a school, although in some respects these are important too. Trying to get a feeling for what relationships are like is a better test of a school. Here are a few things to look out for when assessing whether a school may be right for you.

- **Relationships between teachers and pupils** – these are the life-blood of a school. Unless teachers are enjoying what they do with the people they are trying so hard to motivate and inspire, they'll struggle to raise attainment and will soon feel the whole thing is pointless. Look closely at whether:
  - teachers seem to be enjoying themselves when they teach
  - teachers speak to children and students with respect and courtesy. There are bound to be a few lapses, but what is the general tenor?
  - children and students speak and listen to teachers with courtesy and respect. Are they listening attentively? Are they engaged? Or do they answer back? Or show dumb insolence when spoken to – silent but sullen?
  - support staff are treated with respect by teachers and students; or is their contribution given short shrift and their authority not recognised?

- **The atmosphere and movement around the school** – do the children and students:
  - dash about pushing and shoving each other? Or is there a reason-able degree of orderliness given these are young people with a lot of energy?
  - seem reasonably eager to get back to their classes, or do they take a long time to come in from breaks?
  - take a long time to settle down, or do they settle in well and quickly to the lessons, especially if they are moving rooms (as is the case in secondary schools)?
  - inspire from the teachers – is their focus on learning? or on maintaining discipline?

- **Relationships between students** – try to get a feel for whether the students:

  ○ enjoy school and are having fun learning

  ○ play and co-operate with each other in the playground and classrooms

  ○ see bullying and gangs as a major problem.

- **Relationships between teachers** – observe whether:

  ○ teachers seem to be having fun with each other – is the atmosphere in the staff room light and breezy? Do people have a sense of humour?

  ○ teachers spend time talking in a supportive manner with each other – do they share problems, help and advise each other, talk professionally about the job and the children?

  ○ teachers spend much time in the staff room – do they use it to relax, chat and discuss a range of things over coffee, as well as rushing around preparing and marking? Or is it a place no-one ever goes to?

  ○ staff turnover is an issue in the school – are you the first appointment made in the last two or three years, or one of a large batch of NQTs who start every September?

The assessment of what is the right school for you is of course very subjective. Don't think that you will automatically be happy at a school with a string of "Outstanding" Ofsted reports, any more than you should avoid a school just out of special measures. The schools in challenging circumstances are often those with the most committed and hard-working teachers, who have an idealistic work ethic second to none and will be of great inspiration as you start your career. Indeed, if you are a really talented and gifted teacher, is it not your professional duty to pit yourself against the biggest challenges that teaching has to offer?

But you will need to bear all these issues in mind without being too judgmental about the school, your prospective colleagues or the children. That's a difficult balance.

For example, the attitudes and behaviour of pupils may be perceived by one person as "cheeky banter" that shows the natural, colourful personality of young people, while for another it may seem inappropriate, disrespectful and even threatening. Only you can really know whether you will feel comfortable and well supported in any given situation.

What kind of school do I want to work in?

The maintained or state sector

The vast majority of teaching opportunities arise in the maintained or state sector. In the UK's maintained sector, there are more than 30,000 schools and 700,000 teachers. Every year, about 25,000 teachers retire and about the same number arrive as new recruits, and that is not counting the number who move between one school and another – so there is a lot of scope to enter the system.

You will need to decide whether working in a particular type of school is an important part of your own selection criteria. Most new teachers seem happy enough just to get their first job offer and tend not to be too picky about whether it is a voluntary-aided faith school or a community comprehensive specialising in media and technology. Nevertheless, it is a factor worthy of some consideration even as you start out, because you will want to feel that the ethos, values and culture of the school fits with your own.

For example, if you are an avowed atheist you may well find the ethos and beliefs of a traditional Roman Catholic school difficult to work with. Your professionalism as a teacher will of course remind you of your duty not to undermine the accepted and established ethos and values of the school – whatever they are – but integrating personal values and professional values can present us all with occasional challenges. You might not think that if you are a PE teacher, for example, it would matter much; but over time you probably will find that unless your personal values and beliefs cohere with those of the school, you'll feel constrained, perhaps even unhappy. Schools are communities after all, with value systems of their own.

There is a bewildering array of types of school in the UK system, ranging from a community primary school with no religious ethos at all to a secondary academy with a strong faith and sponsored by the Church of England. The general character and atmosphere of most schools is similar from one to another in most respects, but there are some cultural and social differences you will notice.

Here are some very broad and general characteristics relating to school governance and location, to compare when you start looking.

Community versus faith

Community schools are provided by, and have their governance overseen by, the local authority, so there is no specific faith characteristic, while admission arrangements are determined by the local authority too. Faith schools – and this can mean Church of England, Roman Catholic, Jewish and to a lesser extent Muslim, Hindu or Sikh – are usually voluntary-aided, which means their governance arrangements allow greater freedom to determine admissions policies and they are free to reflect a specific denominational or religious character in the school ethos.

There is a perception, largely both unfair and inaccurate, that faith schools provide a higher standard of education or stricter discipline than county schools. Even cursory visits, let alone the evidence of Ofsted inspections, would not bear this out. Nevertheless, it survives as a perception in many areas.

A difference you will notice, however, is the character of things such as school assemblies, which in faith schools are of course overtly religious and the religious symbolism, such as crucifixes or religious imagery, is explicit, and sometimes quite widespread throughout the school. If you are not religious or a practising member of the faith of the school, you will probably be asked at interview if you are sympathetic to the school's beliefs, values and ethos. Accepting an appointment in such a school presumes that you would at the very least respect those values and beliefs. Many non-religious teachers feel perfectly at home in faith schools.

Inner-city versus suburban versus rural

These are generalisations of course and some parts of the country clearly buck a national trend, but most schools in the centre of large towns and cities are more socially, ethnically and culturally diverse than those in suburbs and rural areas.

You may be relishing the thought of teaching in a tough inner-city environment. Indeed, the challenge of motivating others may be one of the reasons you decided to be a teacher in the first place. One of the great attractions of teaching in inner-city environments is that you are more likely to be meeting children who are ethnically and culturally very diverse – some of whom will be coming to school fluent in English and two or three other languages, some of whom may have recently arrived from traumatised and war-torn places such as Somalia or Afghanistan, or economically poor places in eastern Europe. Teaching children and students who are multilingual, from a wide variety of different faiths and cultural backgrounds, and who may be dealing with issues such as learning English as a additional language, economic or forced migration, refugee status, poor housing or high unemployment, will all be part of the challenge of teaching in the large towns and cities of modern Britain.

Inner-city schools are still more likely to reflect the diversity of ethnic communities in the UK – particularly African, African-Caribbean and some Asian communities. Many teachers are particularly attracted to teach in inner-city areas for this reason. Such schools provide a rich cultural texture and vibrancy that distinguishes them from most suburban and rural schools.

The picture is changing rapidly, of course, but if teaching children who are socially and economically disadvantaged appeals to you, these days you are just as likely to find them in coastal towns and rural areas as you once were in run-down inner cities. Social deprivation and poverty, measured in schools by the number of children on free school meals, is now acute in places that were once thought of as rural idylls or pleasant seaside towns.

The advice to take from all of this is that you should always visit a particular school and decide for yourself whether you feel comfortable with it – wherever it is and whatever its so-called reputation.

The independent or private sector

While the independent sector, or private sector as it is more commonly known, is much smaller than the state sector – comprising less than 10% of all children at school – it nevertheless attracts many teachers. There are significant pros and cons to teaching in the independent sector.

Pros include:

- generally, you'll teach classes much smaller than those in the state sector

- disruptive behaviour and lack of discipline is likely to be much less of an issue

- pupils and parents might come to school with much greater social capital – such as higher expectations of teaching and academic standards, with connections and financial resources

- school buildings and facilities (such as labs, playing fields and sporting facilities) might be much better resourced

- term times are usually shorter

- there's often more flexibility with curriculum design.

Cons include:

- in some cases, pay and pensions are not as good as in the state sector

- you may be under considerable pressure to perform and achieve specific targets for academic success – both from the school management and directly from the parents

- you may be required to make a considerable commitment to extra-curricular activities in addition to teaching time

- there may be fewer opportunities for job mobility than in the state sector

- you may not have access to the collective support of colleagues through widespread union membership.

Of course, it's a very personal decision, and some of the above might matter little to you either way. Overall, the biggest differences you will notice in independent schools is how the ethos and the culture play a part in the attitude of all those associated with them. Parents, teachers and children are all acutely aware of the keen focus on performance and outcome – but ethos and culture is the X factor in independent schools. They are the characteristics that imbue the sense of entitlement and the confidence that allow privately educated children into powerful and influential networks in wider society. People pay for private education not just for good exam results and access to top universities, but as a way into highly aspirational social and cultural networks.

Teaching in independent schools, therefore, has special and exciting challenges of its own – quite distinct from anything the state sector can offer.

To find out more about schools and teaching in the independent sector, visit the website of the Independent Schools' Council, which represents over 1,200 private schools in the UK: www.isc.co.uk.

How do I apply for a teaching job?

The worst thing about applying for teaching jobs is the laborious process of completing application forms. The public sector generally and schools in particular have for some years become hide-bound by application processes that are dominated either by handwritten paper-based applications or by electronic forms.

The public sector has these systems to ensure good recruitment practices and fair treatment, but it has made applying for teaching jobs arduous, especially when, as a new teacher, you will be applying for tens of them. If you can wade your way through the application process, then the bureaucracy and paperwork of being a teacher will present no problems at all!

However, there are some things you can prepare that will save you time:

1. a cover letter

2. a core supporting (or personal) statement

3. a CV

4. a list of other teaching-related skills, aptitudes and experiences

5. a list of other teaching-related training, courses and qualifications.

Cover letter

This is necessary if your application is directly to the school and may be opened or dealt with by the head teacher or the chair of governors. If your application is to be returned to the human resources department of a local authority, it will more than likely be opened by an anonymous administration assistant, so a personalised letter will be wasting your time.

If it is directly to the school, especially a named person, then address a typed letter to that person saying how excited you are to have the opportunity to apply for that post at that particular school, something like:

"I am very pleased to include my application for the post of Year 5 Teacher at Highgate Junior and Infants School and very feel excited by the opportunity of working there . . ."

List all the items you have enclosed or attached:

- **application form supporting statement**

- **copies of qualifications and certificates**

- **references and testimonials.**

Conclude the letter by saying how much you are looking forward to hearing from them, and end with "Yours sincerely", your signature and your typed name.

A core supporting (or personal) statement

While your supporting statement should be drafted for every different application, it is not always necessary to write an entirely new application for each job as you enter the profession. As an NQT, you are not applying for a post with particular responsibilities such as literacy co-ordinator or head of year, so the person specification you will be working to will be very similar from one job to the next.

Obviously, each one will vary to some degree (for example, one primary school might be looking for a Year 3 teacher and another a Year 5), but you will be able to draft the core of a supporting statement that can be easily adapted and amended from one specification to the next.

Read the job description carefully for the role, tasks and responsibilities you will be expected to carry out. However, it is the applicant specification that is the key issue for all job applications.

The applicant specification is the employer's wish list of personal attributes for the successful candidate. It will seek to match things such as:

- qualifications

- skills

- knowledge

- experience

- attitude and personality and interests

to the person applying and the business needs of the post.

While of course it should be true and factual, you are writing this to *persuade* the reader that you are the best person for this post, so it is not a list (as your CV should be – see below).

Give your personal statement some structure, targeting the key words in both the job description and desired attributes listed.

- Start with a paragraph of general introduction about how you think your skills and aptitudes are an excellent fit for this post.

- Then address the applicant specification directly and systematically.

- Some people will do that point by point and in sequential order, giving examples using the "STAR" approach of how they responded to a

  ○ *situation* with a

  ○ *task* and an

  ○ *action* that had a positive (or even not so positive)

  ○ *result*.

- This method can appear a bit dry and boring and could result in a long supporting statement, though, so be careful.

- Other people prefer to write a narrative that covers all the requirements by describing a series of scenarios. If you are confident about your writing ability then this may be more compelling.

- You could call the school and ask whether it has a preference for the way supporting statements are set out. But however you do it, you should read it out loud to a friend or relative and make sure you have described *in yourself* all the qualities, skills, competencies and experiences the school requires.

- Endings are very important, so try to end with a zing – say something that will show your energy and enthusiasm, something such as: "I genuinely feel that my skills, personality and experiences to date are ideally matched for the post and I am incredibly excited about the prospect of starting my career at your school . . ."

If the school is looking for a Year 3 teacher who has an interest in maths, don't keep banging on about what a brilliant science project you did on your final teaching practice with a Year 6 class. It will do you no good at all and will only ensure your application is binned. You will have to draw on whatever relevant and appropriate skills you have developed in maths, and elaborate positively on the experiences you have had with younger children doing maths on previous teaching practices, even if it wasn't with a Year 3 class.

Don't hide your light behind a bushel either. You will need to talk up and highlight every experience as though it were life-changing and filled you with confidence, but balance that with not sounding big-headed and boastful. However, it's fine to say "I believe I have acquired excellent numeracy teaching skills from the regular small group sessions I did with under-achieving boys . . ." or "I am convinced I have the confidence and personality to adapt easily to working with Year 3 . . ."

Just make sure that everything you say addresses that applicant specification directly because that's what they will be checking against.

Most applications these days are done electronically, so you can edit, amend and tweak your supporting statement each time you apply, and copy and paste amendments into the relevant boxes. (A word about fonts, though – keep it smart, traditional and don't use Comic Sans.)

A CV

You will soon lose the will to live if you are writing or typing out your CV from scratch every time you apply for a job – especially as this really is a very boring administrative task. Your CV is simply a factual list consisting of:

- **personal details:** your full name, home address, contact details including phone and email address, and your Teacher Reference Number (often known as your DfE number)

- **employment history:** your previous jobs, with details of post held, dates started and finished, employers' names and addresses

- **education and qualifications:** list your schools, colleges and universities, the dates and exam passes, grades and degree class.

If you have this saved as a Word document, you can readily add and amend it, then copy and paste on an electronic application or simply print a copy to attach it to a paper version.

A list of other teaching-related skills, aptitudes and experiences

This list might include things such as :

- "I am the Youth Racing and Training Officer for my local sailing club"

- "I play acoustic guitar to Grade 4"

- "I teach English conversation classes as a volunteer to new immigrants at my local women's centre"

- "I am the treasurer of my church choir".

A list of other teaching-related training, courses and qualifications

These include things you may have done prior to teacher training:

- "I am a trained first aider and have First Aid at Work certificates"

- "I have an NVQ Level 2 in Retail Management"

- "I completed a creative writing course at my local evening institute".

When you become a qualified teacher, update these lists on a regular basis. As a new teacher, you will be doing a lot of professional development courses in the first few years on the job. You will want to show how valuable and relevant these are when applying for your first promotion.

Reflections from the newteachersblogger – newteachersblog.wordpress.com

Have you got a criminal conviction or caution? Does it make you unsuitable to teach?

Sometimes students and trainees ask me whether having a criminal record is a bar to teaching. The answer, you may be surprised to learn, is usually no. But it depends what the conviction is.

A lot of people get worried that something as trivial as speeding points on your driving licence might be a problem – which of course it isn't. If we barred every teacher who had been banned for speeding, let alone having three points on their licence, we'd have a major crisis in teacher recruitment!

However, teaching is exempt from the Rehabilitation of Offenders Act 1974, and as a teacher, you will be subject to Disclosure and Barring Service

(DBS) checks (formerly known as Criminal Records Bureau or CRB checks). As most people on teacher training courses have already declared their previous criminal convictions and cautions (or should have), and have had a DBS check completed by the university or training provider, this should mean that they have already been deemed suitable to teach in accordance with guidance laid down by the government through the regulating agency, the National College for Teaching and Leadership.

Of course, candidates with very serious convictions – such as murder, robbery with violence, serious sexual assault, dealing in class A drugs or any at all involving violence against children or vulnerable adults – would normally have been weeded out as "unsuitable" at an initial DBS check.

Some, though, even those as serious as manslaughter in situations deemed self-defence, given the circumstances, might not necessarily be a reason for barring someone from acceptance on a teacher training course or employment at a school.

However, if you have a conviction or caution of any kind, what will worry you is how training providers and schools that you will be applying to will view your application.

Minor convictions are almost always not considered serious enough to deem a person unsuitable for teaching. If someone has been foolish in their youth and has been convicted of drug possession, a minor burglary, theft of a car or from a store, a minor affray at a football match or political demonstration, they probably have no need to worry about it affecting their chances of becoming a teacher.

Of course, any convictions that included violence against a person are taken very much more seriously; but still, the circumstances and history of the offence would be the issue taken into consideration.

A trainee asked me recently whether a conviction for a domestic violence incident would count against him. It involved threatening his former wife with a knife when he was drunk and distraught more than a decade ago.

He had declared it to the university but was worried now that he was applying to schools. I suggested to him that most people have a very forgiving nature, given the circumstances. What I couldn't guarantee was that every member, of every selection panel, of every school that he might apply to, would react so forgivingly to such an incident.

It is always difficult to know how people on interview panels will react to a given issue, especially where parent governors are present, as they invariably will be. It won't help that schools are likely to receive scores of applications for every post they advertise so they can pick and choose — it is a buyers' market.

But there's no need to despair completely. Many people, including head teachers and parent governors, do not view "a misspent youth" as necessarily a bad thing. In my experience, many governors even think a little bit of "life experience" helps teachers relate more empathetically to pupils and students, particularly those disaffected with education and demonstrating challenging behaviour.

Depending on what the issue is, you may even be wise to bring it out into the open at interview — explaining to the panel how you mended your ways and used the experience as a catalyst to make you a more reflective and mature person. In my view, that approach is far better than leaving it as the elephant in the room.

When I was a primary head teacher, I employed a man who had an historic conviction for a drunken assault at a football match. He went on to become the most popular teacher in the school with both pupils and parents.

The point is, whatever the conviction or caution, declare it. If you don't, that in itself is reason for summary dismissal.

If you want to know more about what convictions might be deemed unsuitable to be a teacher, you can go to www.gov.uk/disclosure-barring-service-check for more information.

Alternatively, if you have joined a union as a teacher trainee – and my advice is you that you should – then consult them. For instance, the National Union of Teachers (NUT) has a very useful fact sheet on this: www. teachers.org.uk/files/crb-checks—faqs.doc?

Preparing for interview

When you see a job that you want to apply for, there are a number of things you should do to prepare for interview, if and when you get the call.

- **Keep the advert:** bookmark it or, better still, print it out if it is online, or keep the press cutting. Keep in mind what the advert said – it may reveal something that is not in the job description or the person specification, such as "Energetic and resourceful teacher required for lively but loveable class". This could be code for "You'll need the patience of a saint to teach this lot!"

- **Read the school's website:** this will at least provide you with basic information about the school and will include the latest Ofsted report (which is important, but shouldn't sway your opinion too much – an "Outstanding" rating from Ofsted does not necessarily mean you will be happy or well-supported there). Keep in mind that most of the information is designed to get parents to send their children to the school, so there will be an inevitable gloss.

- **Read the DfE information about the school:** this will give you another dimension, as it will offer comparisons with schools of a similar profile, absence rates, trends in performance and so on. Look for the school at www.education.gov.uk/schools/performance.

- **Visit the school:** prior to interview if possible. Get a feel for the children, the staff, the building and the local area. For first appointments, the school may arrange a group visit with other applicants. Don't be intimidated by that – go and see what you make of it. Many schools will discourage individual pre-visits on the grounds of equal opportunities, but give all candidates who are short-listed a full tour on the day of interview.

- While you're there, take a walk around the area and pick up on the vibe. Go into a few local shops such as newsagents and estate agents, and say you are thinking of moving to the area and want to know what the local schools are like. See whether you can glean something about the general perception of the school.

- **Prepare a list of possible questions:** and make some rough draft answers – not to learn verbatim, but just so you have the outline of a good answer in your head. You'll get be asked things such as these:

  ○ describe what you think good teaching is

  ○ describe what kind of teacher you are

  ○ tell us about your most successful lesson or lessons while on teaching practice

  ○ what are your strongest teaching skills?

  ○ what would you admit to as your weaknesses?

  ○ describe how you would deal with disruptive behaviour in class

  ○ describe how you would deal with a child reporting to you that they have been bullied

  ○ what particular skills and attributes will you bring to the school?

  ○ how will you differentiate your lesson planning for children with widely varying abilities?

  ○ do you have any sporting, musical or other extra-curricular interests and abilities you could offer?

- Don't try to learn your answers off by heart. Instead, rehearse them by going through them aloud with a friend or relative, so you can hear yourself, your tone and the pace of your delivery.

On the day

Of course, you will be nervous, but so will everyone else, and the head teacher, senior staff and governors will be aware of that and should be re-assuring and sympathetic. Unfortunately, it's likely to be gruelling, because these days even interviews for NQTs can take up half a day or longer, and any of the following may be part of the process.:

- **You may be given a tour of the school,** often by a group of children or with a member of the governing body not involved in interviews. Just smile at everyone, comment favourably on nice displays and put up with it – what you say at this stage won't matter a jot, unless you start swearing like a trooper...!

- **You'll be introduced to the teachers and other staff,** perhaps over coffee at break-time or over sandwiches at lunch. Usually they haven't got much time to speak to you, but nevertheless, be as friendly as you can even in the brief moments you'll have with them. If they do make time to meet you or talk with you, don't ask "What's it like to work here?" or "Is the head good?" – you won't get an honest answer anyway. But if you ask "What do you like about working here?", you might find out something interesting that will inform your answers at interview.

- **You may be "interviewed" by a group of children or students.** These will be children selected from the school council, and usually accompanied by a teacher or governor. This can be good fun and again, it's an opportunity to show your personality and how much you like kids – but even if they report to the interview panel, don't think it will make much difference to the final decision. It won't.

- **You may be given lunch with the children or students in the school dining room:** this will tell you more about the school than the website, brochures or Ofsted reports, so take note. The atmosphere of a school during lunch-time – particularly the behaviour on display, both good and bad – is a great indicator of the real character of a school.

- **You may be shown some exemplary teaching,** usually that of a senior teacher rather than a tour of the school where every class is disturbed.

This might give you a general idea of the state of relations between teachers and children in the school, although they are hardly likely to show you a teacher struggling to cope with a raucous class. If they do, you may want to politely make an excuse to leave there and then . . .!

- **You may be asked to teach.** This is very common these days and, if asked, meet that request with enthusiasm. It is, after all, what you've applied to do. Even if you are terrified, try to show that you actually like children and try to look as though you are having fun. Show some energy without generating gratuitous excitement. All the usual rules that you have learned on teaching practice apply, so make sure you:

  o have all the resources you'll need without asking the school to supply any

  o maintain control – this is not a jolly but a demonstration lesson

  o manage your time – finishing a few minutes early will not throw you as much as being interrupted for over-running.

- **You will be interviewed . . . finally!** Many schools will involve as many school governors as possible and so some panels will have up to eight or ten interviewers, even for an NQT position, although it's unlikely they will all ask questions. If the school is sensible, they'll keep the panel to four or five people maximum, including the chair of governors and the head teacher in a primary school, or the school's deputy head and chair of the recruitment and appointments committee if it is a large secondary.

Making a success of the interview

Don't be discouraged by the number of interviews you may have without being offered a job. It's not unusual these days to interview for scores of jobs before securing a place, but there are some things you can do that will maximise your chances and eliminate some of the liabilities.

- **Dress and appearance:** you don't have to look like a City banker, but do turn up looking smart and well groomed. Comb your hair, shine your shoes and make sure your fingernails are clean. If you have any tattoos or body piercings, cover them. If you are being interviewed on a warm summer's day, don't wear revealing tops, short skirts, shorts, T-shirts. Remember this is an interview you want to succeed at, not a test of moral and personal values – whether yours or other people's.

- **Your face and eye contact:** when you enter the room, let your smiling eyes do the talking. While you are being settled and introduced to the panel, do a bit of scanning and skimming – that is to say, run your gaze from left to right and back again. As you scan the members of the panel, also skim, like a stone across a pond, to engage people individually by looking directly into their eyes. When they start asking questions, be conscious of your eye contact, and direct your main focus straight back at the questioner.

- **Your posture:** sit up in the chair, cross your legs if you are comfortable that way and have your hands on your lap. Try to look relaxed but engaged and alert.

- **Answer the question:** make sure you answer the question you have been asked and don't ramble off the topic. If you can, answer questions using three short points or examples – it has more impact that way.

- **Make sure your answers are well practised:** rehearse with your family or friends the night before the interview. There's no point in honing your theoretical answers to perfection if you fail to charm your audience with a lousy delivery on the day.

- **Prepare your questions:** at the end of the interview, the chair of the panel will ask if you have any questions. Prepare one or two, perhaps with supplementaries. This would be a good time to ask, in a courteous and respectful tone, if you were to be offered the post, what kind of support you would get during your induction year? (See also the section "What support can I expect during my first, induction year?", p.171 below, for more on this).

Remember the old business adage that "People Buy People" – there's no better way of gaining the confidence of others than fixing their gaze and charming them with a lovely smile. It's how people fall in love after all. Make them fall in love with you!

After the interview, all the candidates may be asked to wait for the result. If so, this will be excruciating as you will probably be asked to wait with everyone else in a room until a member of the panel comes in and takes one of you back to the panel to be offered the job. If it's you, they will expect you to accept it on the spot.

If you find that you don't want the job after the interview, say so immediately and explain the reasons why, if you can. This is not easy, but it will minimise the damage if you tell them right away that you have had second thoughts and "though the school is lovely, the job just doesn't feel right for me."

If you accept the job and then change your mind a few days or weeks later, everyone will feel you have wasted their time. If you go back on an oral agreement because you have been waiting to see if you get a "better" job at another school, they may even be annoyed enough to take civil action.

If you get offered the job, and you take it, ask whether it would be possible to visit the school for a day or two before the end of the summer term and spend some time with your new class or classes, just to observe. It would give you the chance to get a feel for the place and how the children or students are responding, meet some new colleagues and get to know the routines – that way, it won't be such a shock on the first day when the children arrive for the new year.

If you are lucky, you may even be employed (on instructor or unqualified teacher pay rates) for the remaining few weeks of the term in between graduating from your teacher training course and the end of the school term. If you are really lucky, they will pay you over the holidays. Don't try to suggest it to the school yourself – let that initiative come from them, if at all.

Reflections from the newteachersblogger – newteachersblog.wordpress.com

Beginning and ending an interview

Every interview has a beginning, middle and an end, and like every story, the beginning and the end are the most memorable. Make sure you get them right. The really good thing about preparing for the beginning and the end is that you can almost certainly predict what they will be like.

The greeting

You will usually be greeted by someone on the panel, perhaps the head or the chair of governors. Try to have just a little bit of a sense of humour, even at this point. If the head or chair of governors shakes your hand and asks, "How are you?", it's perfectly fine to say, "I'm a nervous wreck actually!", so long as you say it humbly and with a smile.

You can even prepare to make some humorous small talk when you are walking up the corridor to the interview room. A light-hearted introduction will help break the ice and show, paradoxically, that you have confidence.

Besides, self-deprecating humour is both charming and disarming. Just make sure whatever you say is appropriate for an interview!

The first question

The first question at every interview is the one they give to warm you up. It will almost certainly be: "Tell us a little bit about yourself."

With such a gift, you can prepare what you're going to say down to the last detail. Because you should keep your answer reasonably brief, you can and should rehearse it.

Talk about the course at the university or training centre you attended and the things you enjoyed most about the course as well as something personal, such as a love of sport or music, that you pursued or developed while you were there.

If you are a career-changer, give them a brief history of your career so far but, again, include something personal, such as something you enjoy doing things with your family if you have one, or your love of a hobby or pastime.

The final question

One of the biggest mistakes people make at interview is that they don't prepare for the ending. Just imagine – you may have spent an hour or more prior to interview doing various gruelling exercises and activities to test various aptitudes, now you've just got through another 45 minutes or so of answering a range of challenging questions. You have flown your colours from the top of the mast. Then the chair of the panel says, "Do you have any questions for us?" and you say, "Err . . . no, I don't think so . . ."

Wrong!

As this final question is a near certainty, it is something you can really prepare yourself for. Even better, you don't have to answer it, except by turning the tables on your tormentors. Endings create impact and this is your last chance to leave a positive impression.

Be charming. Ask something complimentary. Ask the head or the chair of the panel, in a respectful tone, to give you one sentence about why they are proud of their school. Ask the head, if you were to get the job, what the people you'll be working with are like.

Alternatively, or additionally, you could ask something philosophical. Ask the head, "What's your philosophy of education?" or ask the chair of the panel, "What's your idea of an ideal school, and how far do you think you have got towards that ideal with this school?" Again, make sure your tone is right.

Such questions will again show your confidence and assurance. Since your interviewers will probably be meeting lots of candidates, you should not miss this opportunity to ask such a question and make yourself stand out.

On your way out

Don't forget to smile and thank them for their time. When you leave, the panel will be talking about you, of course. They'll be filling out forms, ticking boxes and grading your experience, qualifications, communication skills and, more than they will be allowed to admit, your personality.

The reality, whatever interviewers say about impartiality, equal opportunities and equity, is that their decision will not just be informed by how experienced and well qualified you are, but also how memorable you are.

With some preparation on the questions you know for certain will come your way, that memorable person can be you.

Good luck!

What support can I expect during my first, induction year?

This is a very important question for you to bear in mind when choosing your first job: what will your first year be like, and how well will you be supported during it? We will also deal with this in some detail in the next chapter, but it's a question you should not forget to ask, especially if you are offered the job at interview. Before you accept, make sure you ask:

- will the school be able to commit to fully supporting your induction programme

- (in other words, does the school have the resources to support me fully)?

- how much non-contact time can I expect during my induction programme? (it should be at least 20%)

- what will happen if other teachers are absent on the days I am due non-contact time; will I have to forgo it?

- does the school have an induction programme run in collaboration with other schools or the local authority (in other words, will I be able to meet other teachers in my position)?

- who will be my mentor during my induction programme, and how often can I expect to meet with them formally to review and record my progress?

Getting some commitment to these issues before you accept the post formally is important. At interview, you will have had witnesses. Promises made later by a busy head teacher in a rushed phone call may sadly, although not intentionally, be forgotten.

11

Life in the classroom

Nothing prepares you for the reality of taking your own class for the first time. Not even long teaching practices where you have been left to fend for yourself. It's like a conductor standing in front of an orchestra — you are directing the score, but you can't be sure that all the players will follow your directions! The crucial difference between teaching practices and taking your own class is that *you* will be the one responsible for teaching a class of 30 children for the first time in a way that, up until now, has not been the case. When you take over a class *you* are the one responsible, not just for teaching and educating them, but also for their welfare and safety. Accepting that responsibility with all its weight and complexity is one of the reasons teaching *is* a profession and not just a job.

It will be a shock to your system, although the shock will perhaps be slightly less if you have taken a school- or employment-based route into teaching, such as a School Direct or SCITT course, where your teaching responsibilities have been gradually measured out to you.

Nevertheless, that first day, when the children come into the room for the first time and you realise you are their teacher, is one that you won't forget for a very long time. It is a day when you will feel an enormous sense of trepidation and excitement – but the more you prepare, the more you'll feel ready for the experience, be able to enjoy it and cope with the unforeseen circumstances if and when they happen.

Before the new term starts

Some new teachers think that they need to spend all summer preparing lesson plans and resources – if you do, you'll be a nervous wreck before you start. Make sure you take a really good, relaxing and distracting holiday after you have completed training, and reward yourself a little if you have any money left at the end of the course – you have earned it after all. Whatever you do, come back feeling refreshed and rejuvenated and ready for the challenge.

A couple of weeks before the new term begins, start to get your thoughts in order about how you are going to manage the first few weeks. Any new job requires a period of preparation and settling in. The problem you have in teaching is that children and students don't know and don't care about any of that! They will expect you to be their teacher from day one and so you will have to be as confident and as well prepared as if you were an actor going on stage for the first time. The audience don't know if this is your first performance. They have paid their money and they want value. So be ready.

By this time, you will almost certainly know which classes and year groups you have been allocated – especially if you are a primary teacher. If you are in secondary, you may have to wait just before the start of term before you get a detailed idea of your timetable, but, with any luck, the school will have given you a good idea of the bulk of your teaching and pastoral responsibilities.

The training or INSET day

All schools start the autumn term with a In-Service Education and Training, or INSET day for all staff. These training days – and there are at least five of them a year – are usually about some general professional development matters that bring all the staff together. They might be changes in education policy, the exams regime or the National Curriculum that must be accommodated. Sometimes, the day will be divided between meetings on topics such as these, followed by phase or departmental meetings that may be more specific to you or the department's needs. Sometimes, outside trainers and speakers are brought in for some specific issue, such as improving provision for children with special needs in mainstream classes, or how to respond more effectively to challenging behaviour. If the speakers are engaging and entertaining, this may be the most interesting part of the day.

Obviously this will be a good opportunity to meet your new colleagues in an atmosphere that, while professional, will be relatively relaxed, so you won't need to dress smartly for this day (smart-casual would be the normal dress code). A word of caution: don't appear too opinionated at this stage, even if you hear or see things you don't particularly like or agree with. You won't make many friends if your new colleagues think you are full of yourself. Being a bit cocky would not make a good first impression.

However, for an NQT, making some early alliances with other new teachers in the first couple of years of work is a good idea. Seek them out.

Above all, try to make time for having coffee or lunch with your induction mentor – this is likely to be the key working relationship you will have over the next year. They will be your conduit to so many sources of communication and support, both within and outside the school. If it works well, you will be able to confide all your mistakes, fears and doubts in them; so it is important that you get on with this person.

You will almost certainly be allowed to spend a few days in school getting ready ahead of the start of term. A week or so before you even get into school, start to put together a list of things you can do when you get there. If you know you will have your own classroom, for example, as you will in nursery and primary schools, get in there, sort it out and put your own personality and mark on it.

- **Clear everything that the previous teacher has left for you to sort out or get rid of – you may need to tidy the detritus of a desk drawer or cupboards full of books, folders or scrap paper, and sometimes just junk.**

- Arrange the desks and chairs the way you want the children or students to sit — don't leave it to the children or students to choose.

- Get your own resources ready and have them to hand — your own pens, markers, stationery, IT equipment and so on, so you are not flustered when that first lesson gets under way.

- Label resources, cupboard doors, shelves and trays with children's names if you are in nursery or primary school.

- Put up some "Welcome" signs, interesting posters or display materials until the children and students produce some work that you can exhibit.

- Get teaching resources such as text books, exercise books and writing materials ready for distribution (but be careful not to raid the school stock cupboards without talking to responsible senior staff or teaching assistants first— otherwise you'll be in trouble before you start!)

- Prepare your class lists and registers and learn some names — it'll help when you start putting a face to them. Getting to know names early on is an effective technique for managing people — it makes them feel special.

- Get yourself a folder for your own essential documents, such as your timetable, class lists, lists of children with special needs, lessons and weekly plans.

- Prepare folders for the other stuff that you don't need on a day-to-day basis but which is important — such as half-termly or termly schemes of work or whole-school policies on behaviour, for example — and if you don't have a desk in the room, at least make some space for yourself on shelves or in cupboards so you know where your own stuff is.

The physical space in teaching, your classroom, is one you must impress yourself on — it is your domain. The more your personality as a teacher is reflected in the room, the more the children will respond to it. You will have much more freedom to do this as a nursery or primary school teacher, of course, but there are opportunities to do it in certain sections of secondary teaching, particularly in areas where you will be teaching in specialist rooms such as studios, labs and suites dedicated to particular subjects.

Other things you might want to do during preparation days before the term starts are to meet with the key people who will be supporting you.

- **Your induction mentor:** your mentor should discuss with you how they will be supporting you, the non-contact time you can expect, and the courses and development days scheduled as part of the induction programme that you can expect to attend. Get some regular induction review meetings put into both your diaries.

- **The head of department (in secondary):** this is the person responsible for the direction, resourcing and quality of teaching in the department within which you are teaching, so it's important you have a good working and personal relationship with them. If they are any good, they will be an important factor in the way your career is supported and fostered over the first couple of years.

- **The previous teacher of your new class (in primary):** the most important thing here is to have a good conversation with this person about each child in your new class (if they are still working in the school, that is). This person will give you the background and specifics about all the children in your class, particularly those about whom you may need to know pertinent information such as whether they have special needs or unusual personal circumstances, in "Looked After" care or with parents who are military personnel and so on.

- However, be careful to keep an open mind about children. The way they respond to one teacher can be entirely different to another. A little devil with one teacher can be an angel with another.

- **The head of year (in secondary):** again, this may be an important strategic alliance for you, especially in terms of background information and liaising over the pastoral needs or the behaviour and discipline of students.

- **TAs you may be working with:** good TAs are worth their weight in gold. They can take huge loads off your shoulders as well as finding a personal touch or creative ways of making connections with pupils and parents, perhaps communicating with them in a different style to teachers. Don't underestimate the demands on your time and energy that may be required in managing TAs effectively, though. On the one hand, they will look to you for clear and unambiguous direction for defining the scope of teaching content. On the other, if they have been at the school for many years, they know it all!

- **The special educational needs co-ordinator (known as the SENCO):** this is another important relationship to foster, especially where you have children with statements of special educational need in your class – that is, where children have both resources and a defined programme for addressing issues affecting their learning. The SENCO will be an experienced teacher who should be a source of advice, support and access to additional resources to help you do your job effectively with the children you teach that are on the special educational needs (SEN) register.

Take a walk around the school site and familiarise yourself with the classrooms, assembly halls, stock cupboards, toilets (both staff and pupil) and the layout of corridors and hallways. If it is a secondary school, it may be a very large site, with labs and sports halls, and you'll need to set aside quite a bit of time for this. But it will be a good way of introducing yourself to people from whom you will certainly need support at some point in the near future, for example:

- the school secretary, office administration assistants or PA to the head teacher

- the school caretaker and site managers

- the school cook and dinner ladies

- technicians and reprographics staff.

In getting yourself ready for the start, you will almost certainly over-plan and over-prepare for your first few days and weeks. Not to worry. You will soon realise that teaching is an art as well as a science. The important thing is that you *do* plan and prepare – winging it for the first few days to see how the kids respond is not an option you should consider, however confident and brilliant you think you are.

While planning and preparation is essential to give yourself a confident start, perhaps at least as important is allowing time to think about how you will project a confident persona in the first crucial hours and days. Confidence is absolutely essential if you are to function effectively as a teacher, and this will be tested, almost forensically, when you start with a new class.

Reflections from the newteachersblogger – newteachersblog.wordpress.com
Learning from your mistakes

As a new teacher, you'll make lots (and lots) of mistakes. Don't worry about it. You'll not only survive them, you'll learn from them; and if you reflect on them honestly, you'll be a better teacher for them too.

Most mistakes will be small and inconsequential, such as losing a child's homework or confusing the names of twins. The kids won't care, so neither should you. "Learn from your mistakes" should be a maxim for teachers and children alike.

Occasionally, though, you'll make a bad mistake and wonder why you ever wanted to teach in the first place, have a sleepless night about it and think that your fledgling teaching career lies in tatters on the classroom floor.

Don't.

Mistakes are a natural part of learning. If you never make mistakes, you're not trying hard enough or taking the risks necessary to become the teacher you deserve to be.

There are very few mistakes you can't recover from. Even bad ones.

Here's my evidence:

My first year in teaching was with a difficult Year 6 class; at least, I thought so at the time. Trying to get them to line up for assembly, leave the classroom in an orderly manner or raise their hand before shouting out answers was my daily diet of psychological torture.

To my mind, water-boarding ran only a close second to the turmoil I endured taking the kids to the weekly swimming lesson at the local pool. First, the school bus driver gave me withering looks at my lack of natural authority with them. Then when we got there, the kids made a habit of mischievously jumping straight into the pool as soon as they were changed. So the swimming instructor would start the lesson by bawling at them at the top of his voice what "hopeless, useless articles" they were, but all the time looking straight at me.

One week, I made an issue of warning the kids not to jump in the pool before the lesson began. I warned them in the classroom before we left school. I warned them on the bus on the way to the pool. And I warned them again as we entered the changing rooms.

I think you know what's coming . . .

Sure enough, within seconds of me going into the changing room and starting to change myself, I heard the delighted shouts and screams of children jumping in the water. By the time I opened the changing room door, more than half a dozen were already splashing about laughing and giggling.

I flipped.

"Right! That's it!" I shouted at the whole class, including the 20 or so assembled innocently sitting at the side of the pool, "Out! Everybody out! Everybody get changed right now! We are not having another swimming lesson until you can all learn how to behave yourselves properly . . . blah, blah, blah . . ."

They weren't listening. The mood changed instantly. A sombre, seething pall of anger, bitterness, even hatred, exuded from them at the naked injustice of a collective act of punishment. There was total silence getting changed and getting back on the bus, for once.

But it doesn't take long before children start singing songs on buses. This one was a simple, well-known refrain. You probably know the tune – sing along if you like. It goes like this . . .

"We hate you Newland . . . we do! We hate you Newland . . . we do!

"We hate you Newland . . . we do! Oh Newland, WE HATE YOU!"

I think, by the sound of it, every child on the bus was singing it at the top of their voice.

That night, I went home exhausted, hating school, hating teaching and, I admit it, hating those kids. I was convinced they had it in for me. The little swines, as I thought of them that night, had ground my lofty idealism to dust in the space of a few months. After an almost sleepless night, I got up the next morning with a foreboding dread, wondering what new tortures awaited me.

On the bus to school, I dreamed longingly of being a shelf-stacker at Sainsbury's . . .

Over a coffee in the staff room I confided the incident to the worldly but sympathetic ear of my colleague Olive, a hugely talented and experienced Reception-class teacher. She gave me a forgiving look and said, "When you go in there this morning, tell the whole class you are going to do two things. First, you are going to apologise to all those children whom you punished who didn't deserve to miss their swimming lesson. Secondly, but without any tone of threat, just tell them that you'll do exactly the same thing next week, and every week, until they all get the message."

I did what she said. Next week went like a dream. They had learned a lesson. I felt like a teacher in command.

And though I made many more mistakes that year . . . I had learned an important lesson too.

Your first days, weeks and months

First impressions

- Look and feel smart: you don't have to wear Paul Smith or Ted Baker, but get yourself into the mentality of looking and feeling professional and stylish in both appearance and manner. This is for your benefit as much as the way the students and your colleagues perceive you.

- When children or students walk in the door, greet them courteously and warmly but not effusively – remember you are their teacher, not their friend. You are there to do the business of teaching and learning – so no high-fives or "Hi guys! How was your summer?"

- You don't have to be Lord Sugar in his boardroom, but maintaining a certain distance and even the sense that you are an unknown quantity will be to your advantage at this stage. Remember that aphorisms such as "Familiarity breeds contempt" were coined for a reason – because they are true!

- Set out the ground rules immediately, without sounding authoritarian or unfriendly. Before you start any teaching remind them about your expectations of the classroom and the school's golden rules for behaviour, while attracting attention and moving around the room. Your consistency in keeping to these rules, and reminding them when necessary, will be the crucial factor in the first few hours, days and weeks.

- Don't "chase" them: new teachers will soon find themselves chasing various goals on the teaching agenda, including the initial acceptance of getting pupils quiet and listening to what you have to say. Some experienced teachers will advise you to "Wait for complete silence before you begin to speak". Others will say: "If I waited for every child to be silent before I began, I'd be there all day." This is a difficult one – and you will have to find your own effective style – but waiting for every single child to be silent before you start to speak frustrates (and soon alienates) the well-behaved kids who are already sitting quietly waiting for you to begin. It also hands a lot of power to those kids seeking attention. You may find that getting the attention of 90% is enough to launch in to what you have to say, and you can then bring the stragglers into line as you go along.

- Impose your professional personality and charisma: you might have to work on developing this as a particular persona that might not come naturally to you at first, but it is important that you do so. Pupils expect you to have it. If you think you will survive in teaching because children will respond to you as the nice person you are, forget it. The persona you need to project primarily to carry out your professional role effectively is that of a charismatic, professional teacher – when they see you can effectively project that, then they will also respond to you as the nice person you undoubtedly are.

- "Accentuate the positive, eliminate the negative" are lines from the classic song covered by every crooner from Bing Crosby to Paul McCartney. The reason it's a classic? It's a great song and it works. The maxim should underpin your philosophy for managing the behaviour of children and young people, from day one to the day you retire.

Week one and beyond

You won't be wearing a big yellow life-jacket with your hand poised to jerk the inflator cord, but you will be in survival mode during your first week or two. Like those trained in survival techniques, your life should be characterised by these strict routines:

- get up early and give yourself plenty of time to get ready

- eat breakfast at home: porridge, a banana, toast or some other slow-release energy-provider, if it's good enough for marathon runners, it's good enough for new teachers. Don't miss breakfast and end up snacking on high-energy, high-caffeine junk by mid-morning

- get into school early and give yourself an organised start without rushing round too much

- teach your lessons (this may be the least of your problems!)

- eat fresh fruit at lunchtime: apples are especially good for an energy boost; don't eat too many carbohydrates such as sandwiches or chips, you'll only feel sleepy in the afternoon

- after lunch: teach more lessons!

- after school: don't slump into a chair in the staff room and fall asleep, get a quick tea or coffee and get on ... plan, prepare (and mark if appropriate) for the next day

- go home, prepare, cook and eat some fresh and nutritious food; try to relax around a meal

- spend some time reflecting on your day and evaluating the pros and cons, fill in any gaps in your planning and prepare for the next day

- stop whatever you are doing, work-wise, by 10p.m. at the latest

- watch a little TV, listen to music, phone a friend or just go to bed early and read a novel, but whatever you do ...

- be in bed by 11p.m. and try to sleep.

This should be your defined routine for the first few weeks. If you keep yourself up all night worrying about how much planning you need to do for the next day, you will be a wreck by the end of the first fortnight. Keep to this routine – as a strict regime – for the first few weeks or until half term, or at least until you start to feel you have some regular, patterned behaviours in place. You won't be the worst teacher in the world (or the first!) if you go into a few lessons feeling under-prepared. Much better to feel under-prepared but fresh for the next day than over-prepared and too tired to project that charismatic personality you have been working hard to hone.

Your first month or two

Very quickly, you will start to feel as though you are getting the hang of it, especially if you are preparing efficiently, eating and sleeping regularly and have adopted the first impression and strict routine advice.

Your colleagues, even your induction mentor, will probably have left you to settle in during the first week or so. They and other supportive colleagues will have been asking "How are things going?" every so often, to be reassuring. But as the weeks go by, you will need to establish your support networks and be systematic about nurturing some of them.

- Meet regularly with your induction mentor – quite often people in this role turn out to be some of the most experienced teachers in the school, often older and certainly wiser. While they may not necessarily be a person you would naturally go for a drink with after work, that doesn't matter. It is a relationship you need to foster and work at because they will have a large bearing on how your induction year is managed and reported. Induction is something that you must pass, and although extremely few people ever fail it, many do struggle, often because this crucial relationship has not served its purpose, or worse, it has broken down.

- On the other hand, the vast majority of induction mentor–mentee relationships are extremely supportive, nurturing and fruitful, and they endure long after the induction year is over. With any luck, your mentor will be a person brimming with ideas, tactics and strategies for coping and thriving as a teacher. More often than not, they will become a sounding board and a confidant for you to offload your doubts, fears and classroom clangers. So try to timetable a series of meetings over the first half term or term – and don't let the daily pressures of work get in the way of them, even if you have an excellent and friendly relationship with your mentor.

- Make friends with colleagues – obviously this is essential, especially if you are the only NQT in the school and don't have natural alliances and confidants to hand. There are always some friendly and sympathetic colleagues, even in the most fraught and stressed of staff rooms. The best way to make friends in school is to go and flatter your departmental colleagues in neighbouring classrooms by saying how nice their room looks, or how you would love to pick their brains for ideas, advice or tips. Don't be afraid to ask silly questions. Just go and "steal" their good ideas – it's a way of complimenting them.

- Soon you be able to confide in them all your mistakes and calamities and feel the better for it. Teaching is a very supportive and collegial profession. Teachers hate seeing their colleagues struggle, not just because of the human empathy that this situation prompts, but because a struggling teacher can turn into a failing teacher very quickly. Failure has implications for the professionalism of everyone, not just you.

- Use wider networks – don't limit yourself to the support systems inside the school alone. If you are in a small primary school, your network of colleagues is unlikely to be sufficient in any case, let alone when you might really need support and good counsel. Here are a few wider networks that you need to establish as the term goes on, if not before it starts:

  o membership of a professional association or union – these will offer dedicated NQT training and development opportunities to their new members, as well as advice and support if the relationship with your induction mentor turns sour. They are also invaluable if you have a genuine grievance with your employer or find yourself the unwitting object of a disciplinary procedure. These are unlikely, of course, but it's a good insurance in today's target-driven culture. But best of all, these organisations offer you a network of other NQTs and teachers with whom you can share ideas and support, not least through online forums the Teacher Support Network – this is an independent charity that provides counselling, information and support on a range of issues that might be affecting you as a new teacher, from the stresses of managing pupil behaviour to help finding accommodation when moving to a new area. Apart from extensive services online they also have a 24-hour helpline where you can talk directly to a trained counsellor; see www.teachersupport.info

  o other online networks include the *Guardian*'s Teacher Network (www. guardian.co.uk/teacher-network), the *TES Connect* online community (http://community.tes.co.uk), or just the informal gathering of thousands of teachers on Twitter every week at #ukedchat.

Even by the end of the first month or so, you will have started to get a real sense of the patterns and rhythms of school days and weeks. You will soon realise how, in a single day, there are intense and busy periods followed almost immediately by just as intense periods of quiet, if not silence. You might find yourself walking around a school and enjoying the almost tranquil air of a place that feels genuinely at ease with itself, where the only sounds are the murmurs or of an organisation focused on the business of teaching and learning, where there is an air of calm and purpose. Suddenly, a bell goes and the atmosphere changes completely. Children flood noisily from classrooms, chatting excitedly, perhaps pushing and shoving on their way to the playground. Teachers quickly reorganise a classroom for a different set of activities, rush out of classrooms carrying piles of books, hurriedly rattle off a conversation with a pupil or a squeeze in a quick meeting with a colleague in what little time is available before the kids come flooding back like a spring tide in full flow.

If you are lucky, there will be the gently echoing sounds of teachers teaching and children learning with an underlying rattle and hum that feels rhythmic. It will be like a tide, with a predictable ebb of intense activity followed by a period of tranquillity, then a flow of yet more intense activity again followed by relative quiet . . . and so on . . . and so on. . .

If you are not so lucky, the atmosphere will feel edgy, raucous and slightly unnerving, where the voices of teachers and pupils are straining and tense, where the ebb and flow is uneven, unbalanced and unpredictable, and where you are never quite sure if the tide will sweep you away uncontrollably and suck you under.

Some schools and some classrooms, even really good ones, go through periods of crisis, and during such periods they know that they are not consistently on top of managing good teaching and learning. But even in schools that feel edgy or even in a crisis, you can thrive as a new teacher if you have good personal support and focus yourself on your teaching and routines. With these structures and habits in place, you will find ways to accommodate the situation, gradually finding your feet and establishing yourself.

There are some patterns in school life that come as a feature of teaching whatever the circumstances. For example, as a primary teacher your work rate in the mornings might feel quite pressured and intense when you are likely to be focusing on literacy and numeracy activities. In comparison, the afternoons – when you are more likely to schedule activities such as PE, games, art or music – might feel comparatively relaxed.

In secondary schools, you might find that all your tough teaching groups, such as those pesky Year 9s and 10s, are all timetabled for the beginning of the week, and gradually you feel more relaxed as the week goes on as you enjoy the comparative innocence and enthusiasm of those sweet little Year 7s on Thursday and Friday afternoons.

These rhythms and patterns you will find reassuring. But be careful not to let early setbacks knock your confidence too much – if that happens, you need to respond with a measured calm, not a state of panic. Do not react to a mini-crisis by dishing out lots of detentions, sending naughty kids to the head or spending all night planning additional activities just because one or two lessons have gone badly. Your response should be to reflect on what you think went wrong and consult with your mentor and other colleagues (such as your head of department or your other NQT colleagues) and compare your analysis with theirs on what went well. Do not be distracted from the focus on your routines – these will get you through those first few weeks and months.

One of the real attractions of teaching is this juxtaposition. On the one hand, the routines of a scheduled timetable with all its predictable rhythms and patterns; on the other, the fresh, often delightful and totally unpredictable discoveries and surprises that punctuate almost every day.

From half term to Christmas

By the time you get to half term you'll feel the need for a reward – and you will have deserved it. By that time, you'll have drawn a couple of months' salary and the world will feel a little better than it did when you graduated your training course with an empty or overdrawn bank account. You'll feel like taking a full-blown week-long holiday in the Mediterranean.

A word of caution: it may not be a wise thing to do at this stage, as it may be too much of a distraction. It's definitely worth going away for the weekend somewhere where you can feel you can forget about school for a couple of days and recharge. If you can't afford that, go for some long walks in the country or treat yourself to a spa or a facial.

Be careful. The half term running up to Christmas can often be characterised by a little over-exuberance and over-confidence on the part of NQTs. Some people make the mistake of taking on additional responsibilities such as helping to run the school football team or helping to organise a school trip planned for the summer. Even worse, they get involved in the Christmas concert or the nativity play. Unless you have direct responsibility for these things (for example, unless you teach in the drama department or are the Reception-class teacher where the nativity play is the annual tradition), then resist the temptation, even if you are having a great half term and things are going swimmingly.

Your colleagues won't think any the less of you, and your mentor should be protecting you from over-work anyway. Just focus on honing your teaching skills and doing the best you can with your own class or classes. Nobody will reasonably expect you to get seriously involved in the wider life of the school before your induction year is complete.

The other thing you will need to keep an eye on during this time is protecting your general health. If you have started burning the candle at both ends, you will find that, as the winter months draw in you, will start feeling listless and exhausted more often. You will have made your body's defences susceptible, and these are ideal conditions for you to pick up a virus. If you end up having a week or two off work with a heavy cold during November or December, this will undermine your confidence much more than a string of difficult lessons. By the time you get back to work, all the routines and ground rules you have painstakingly established will have gone by the wayside and you'll have to start all over again.

Remember those strict routines of early nights and healthy eating. They will protect your health and well-being as they bolster your daily energy needs, so keep to routines!

If you do start feeling run-down and too ill to work, don't think that you are doing anybody any favours if you don't take a day or two off when it's really needed. Teaching, perhaps more than any other profession, is beset by people who think they are heroic and who struggle into school, coughing and spluttering their germs around the place, thinking themselves indispensable, only to find that by the time the holidays finally come, they really do collapse with a serious failure of health.

The second half of the autumn term gets busier and busier with rehearsals for carol concerts, nativity plays, celebrations of various faiths and religious traditions, and often schools are usually decorated to reflect seasonal traditions and religious diversity. The excitement and expectation of the children builds and builds.

This is a time when pupils think they can push the boundaries a little, get a little familiar, jokey, cheeky or so on, and when you yourself might start to think "Oh well, it's nearly Christmas. let's cut them a little slack . . .", letting them take their work or assignments a little less seriously.

Don't.

You won't need to adopt the persona of Ebenezer Scrooge to maintain your focus on good teaching and learning while in the classroom, but if you let your own ground rules slip during this period, you are signalling to your students that you didn't really take them all that seriously in the first place. You will almost certainly live to regret it in January once the Christmassy atmosphere has dissipated.

The atmosphere of a school in December can be very special, particularly in a primary school, and you will be swept up by that growing sense of warmth, wonder and excitement. Enjoy it and get involved; just don't take on huge amounts of extra work or responsibility, and don't let your professional and charismatic persona get diluted or lose its effect. You'll need it again at full strength in January.

Reflections from the newteachersblogger – newteachersblog.wordpress.com

Confessions of a new, young male primary school teacher

Young male teachers sometimes come in for a bit of extra attention from young mums, particularly at primary schools.

Not that I was ever competing with Brad Pitt, but as the only male in the school, I was sometimes the butt of light-hearted flirtatious jokes, and occasional sexualised but harmless banter.

And to be perfectly honest with you, I enjoyed it. I was flattered.

Every Christmas, the school's parent–teacher association organised a highly lucrative Christmas fayre. It was successful in bringing together parents, pupils and teachers in a very convivial way.

There was a range of stalls from tombola to "Bash the Rat" to Santa's grotto, but this year there was also a new one: "A Christmas Kiss under Santa's Mistletoe" where each patron put on a Santa hat, stood under the mistletoe and kissed their chosen person on the cheek – with a snapshot pasted up in a Christmas card as a souvenir to take away.

All good clean fun, although I think you can see where this is going . . .

The stall was attracting hordes of people and making lots of money. Parents kissing their darling little children, children kissing their "Best Mum in the World", proud grandparents with their grandchildren, classmates kissing their best friends . . . This thing was printing money.

Then one or two mums started coming up to me making requests – the kind of request that was difficult to refuse. They wanted to have their picture taken under the mistletoe kissing me. It seemed harmless enough, especially as it was for the school fund. So, under pressure as much from some excited children as the mums, I made the mistake of joking, "Oh all right . . . for the sake of the school fund . . . !"

It was all done in a very jovial way, intended and executed in good fun. But within minutes, there was a line of mums queuing to kiss the only male teacher in the school. Suddenly, there were a lot of mums exclaiming, "Just one kiss for me too . . . !", and sometimes the kisses lasted longer than I would have chosen.

The stall made a lot of money that day. But was I an asset to the coffers of the school? Or had I become a liability to the school's reputation?

The spring term

Most experienced teachers find this the most challenging term of all, and that may be particularly true for your first year in the job. The mornings are dark, damp and miserable, and you spend all day working hard at a physically and emotionally demanding job. Everyone seems tired and hungover after the New Year. The children and students seem to be in school all the time sheltering from the snow or the rain, and suddenly the place makes you feel claustrophobic. By the time you emerge from the building in the late afternoon or early evening, it's dark, damp and miserable again.

By a few weeks into the term, if you are not getting a lot back from the children's enthusiasm for your lessons, the routines you have tried so hard to establish can easily feel like a drag. At this point, you start wondering why you chose to be a teacher . . .

This is the time to refresh.

First, refresh your planning, preparation and teaching and try a few new ideas, particularly those that you didn't have the confidence to try in the first couple of months. Keep to the ground rules and routines, but start taking a few ideas from the schemes of work you used when you were on teaching practice. Try adding a creative and innovative slant to them, but whatever you do, don't tell the children or students that you are going to try something new or "more exciting" – just do it as if it were part of what you had always planned and intended.

With a bit of luck, they will notice a little bit more of a challenge in what you are asking them to do. Don't expect miracles – you are doing this as much to challenge yourself as to challenge them. But the beginning of a new calendar year and the start of the spring term needs a different signal to the one you gave your pupils in September, and a little low-key creativity, innovation or experimentation in your teaching is the right signal to give.

Second, refresh your key working relationships – remember that you need to keep up the regular meetings with your induction co-ordinator and get some written as well as oral feedback. Even if everything is going really well, don't let this slip.

It's *your* induction year, and the non-contact and development time is something you are entitled to. However confident you are feeling, however well lessons and relationships may be going, however many compliments you may be picking up about how brilliant you are, don't fall into the trap of assuming your induction support can be dispensed with.

You can refresh this relationship for the new term by asking your induction mentor to meet at a different day and time or a different location. You could start the meeting by prioritising new issues, focus on developing a set of new teaching techniques or strategies, or analyse and evaluate the learning outcomes of a new group of children. Your induction mentor will have a programme for the year to work through, but should be able to accommodate a new slant on professional goals such as this.

Third, refresh your routines: modify them so you feel that you are controlling them rather than the other way round. Change your breakfast cereal, take different fruit to school each day, take a day a week when you go out of the building and sit in the park for a lunch break. Visit the sales and buy yourself a new outfit to wear for school. Take a regular night off from planning and preparation (or at least finish early) and go out with friends, go to the cinema on Mondays or to the gym or swimming pool on Wednesdays – something nourishing and invigorating, something that will distract you.

But don't abandon your routines, just refresh them for the New Year so that you can restore and protect yourself, physically and emotionally, from the ubiquitous midwinter colds and flu.

Fourth: refresh yourself. Getting to the February half-term break is a major milestone to reach in the marathon that is your first school year. If everything has gone really well and you can afford it, go skiing or do something that exhilarates you. At least go away for a long weekend. If not, do something you can look forward to as the spring arrives, such as planning a holiday for Easter.

After the February half term, if other things are going reasonably well, you will begin to feel you have turned a corner. The ground rules you have established and consistently tried to reinforce with your students will with luck have started to pay off. They will have got the measure of you and you of them. The routines you have established in balancing your own work and personal life should have protected you from the worst effects of stress, exhaustion and illness.

The nights have started to draw out a little, and now when you leave school, it's still daylight! Spring is on its way, and its effects will be felt in your step, both going in and coming out of school with each passing day. Time to look a little further ahead as the Easter holidays approach.

The summer term

As an NQT, you are highly unlikely to be burdened with examination or SAT responsibilities, so you can think of the summer term as a time when you can once again be a little innovative. The brighter and warmer days may provide you with opportunities to enhance teaching and learning by using the school grounds in more flexible ways, particularly with sporting or creative activities. You may feel confident enough to organise short trips out of school, even just locally, to places of interest such as local museums, galleries, woods or even parks and recreation grounds. The science of physics for example – structures, forces, flight – can be enhanced by local visits to bridges, canals, buildings and the construction and testing of paper and model aeroplanes or kites. Biology can be brought to life by working in the school's shrubs or gardens, or by visits studying mini-beasts in local wildlife areas, woods and ponds. Design and technology can be studied in local buildings, engineering, furniture, architecture, fashion; the list goes on. A creative and imaginative teacher can make learning brilliant, exciting and memorable. Of course, visits, even local ones, require thorough and proper planning and full consideration of safety, but the summer term is the ideal time to start.

At the risk of sounding like a stuck record, don't forget your routines. They have sustained you thus far, don't let them go now. But what you can do, if things have gone well, is start to relax them a little.

Summer term is a still a very busy time, and though as an NQT you should be protected from the heaviest of the workloads around SATs or exam preparation, there will still be plenty of other things to do, particularly after half term. You will have reports to write and parents' evenings to prepare for and attend. You'll have sports days and annual outings to help organise. You'll have end-of-term "graduations", celebrations and leavers' parties that you'll need to help with. These are physically demanding and very time-consuming – and they are all in addition to your regular teaching timetable. So don't forget your routines. They are your lifeline.

Case study

Lauren's story

"I'm not just an NQT anymore", explains Lauren Kavanagh.

"As my alarm rings, I have the same debate with myself every morning. Should I get up now at 6.45a.m., or shall I give myself an extra half an hour? I often tend to get out of bed earlier rather than later, as I seem to get more done in the hour before school than I do in an hour after school.

"After preparing all my photocopying for the day and marking some books, having a chat to the other teachers, and of course writing the date on the board, I wait for my class to arrive. Then all us teachers go and stand in the playground to take in the children class by class, in what looks like a police line-up trying to pick out the criminal. I am lucky how welcoming the other members of staff have made me feel and how quickly I have become part of the team.

"While the register is being taken, all the children cannot wait to tell me things they have done the night before or at the weekend. They are so eager and full of life. "Miss, can you say our names in a funny accent?" I do this most mornings. I do it in the afternoon too. It puts us all in a good mood for the day ahead.

"Lessons are like a performance. The children, thirsty for knowledge, hang on your every word. You'll need lots of tricks to keep their attention but sometimes it's the unplanned, spontaneous moments that are the best. Like the time when a child shouted out a shocking comment that resulted in the whole class, including myself crying with laughter. Or the times when I decide, "Right! We're going outside, let's make the most of this weather!"

"Playground duty – Tuesdays and Fridays. Year 5 football, and I have been chosen to referee. Every week we go through the same thing. "Miss, can I be captain and choose my team first?" First I choose two team captains, trying to split up the talented but very competitive footballers, then a quick game of rock, paper, scissors to determine who picks first. Pick a player . . . argue, pick another player . . . argue, finally get the chance to start the game with only five minutes left of playtime . . . argue. I love this time with the children, and wouldn't have it any other way. After a whole year of doing this cycle, we are nearly at no arguments!

"After lunch is the hardest part of the day to organise most of the time, but this can also be the most rewarding and interesting. Topic lessons allow for creativity from both the children and myself: "Miss, how long have we got left until 3.15? I don't want to go home yet."

"The end of the day draws near, and after we have said our prayers we walk downstairs to the playground to meet the parents. This is the best part of the day, not because we are finished (although it is a bonus), but because every child says, "Thank you, Miss, see you tomorrow." At this point, without fail, my heart melts and I am reassured I am 100% in the right job.

"It has been a rollercoaster of emotions this year. Nerves when you first start, along with uncertainty in your capability. But next comes the sense of pride and achievement, when a child grasps a concept *you* have taught them. Then you get overwhelmed halfway through, when people start expecting more because you know the routine. Finally, the end of the school year arrives, and you feel proud and a sense of relief! Proud of the children, proud of yourself for making it to the end without giving up, and proud because you know it has been the best decision you have ever made, to become a teacher and do a job you love."

Induction year case studies

Clare's story

Clare finished her induction year last year.

"I got through my induction year OK, although it's difficult to be always asking for help — even when I really needed it, as my mentor is also very busy and so can't always give me time.

"Having a mentor is very useful, though; it is a real means to improve your practice and becoming a better teacher. In my experience, developing a good and trusting relationship with my mentor was the best way to reflect and develop. They have your best interests, and the best interests of the students, at heart. This does take time though! It can be a tricky relationship at times."

Tommy's story

Tommy, a business studies teacher who did his induction year a couple of years ago, alludes to the pressures of the mentor–mentee relationship.

"I feel that the resources of the school play a key role. I was lucky enough to spend two terms in an outstanding school that was able to send me on numerous continuing professional development (CPD) sessions. However, if you were placed in a struggling school this may not be the case.

"Also, due to the fact the school was judged Outstanding, there was a constant emphasis on the grading of lessons rather than looking at my particular strengths and areas to improve. I felt this slightly demotivating at times, as you felt like being satisfactory wasn't good enough.

"I had two main mentors who had a wealth of experience, and this was very useful. However, during this time (and on my PGCE), I felt that being a mentor was something that some members of staff (in school) did but had a limited amount of motivation for. I feel this can often make the process of asking for advice and receiving feedback very difficult, as they may have more important things to do."

Meena's story

Meena, a secondary music teacher who trained through a school-based route, has had a mixed experience.

"My induction year was quite a contrast to my training school year, providing me with different challenges and development targets. At the training school, there was a very close-knit department, quick to offer support and advice about anything, especially behaviour management and school policy advice.

"Initially at my induction school, I did not feel I received enough support through formal mentor meetings as my head of department and I only have one free period together each week, and she is generally called in for other meetings.

"However, I have slowly been gaining the confidence to ask for more support at other times, and she is very willing to help out. I would say that she is not as inspirational as my training mentor, but she has helped develop my practice in different ways.

"I do feel very valued in the department, despite only being employed on a temporary contract to cover maternity leave. The self-worth they have cultivated in me has encouraged me to retain my independence in developing myself as a teacher and control my own CPD. I now feel settled and very supported and remain motivated."

Charlotte's story

Charlotte, a secondary geography teacher, has had a frustrating induction year in one sense, but within a supportive environment.

"My induction year was not in any way normal. At the time, the department was going through a difficult time due to extenuating circumstances and I, along with another NQT, were left without a head of department for about six to seven months. Rather than having just the normal stresses of a being NQTs, we were suddenly faced with additional responsibilities and tasks that we had not anticipated.

"Despite that, we were still supported by an excellent stand-in head of department and a brilliant temporary NQT mentor, as well as being lucky enough to have four other fellow NQTs there to support us. The support I received both formally and informally was outstanding. There was a real sense of community and when we needed to ask for advice there was always someone there to talk to and nudge us in the right direction."

Andreana's story

Andreana a primary teacher, has had a happy and unproblematic experience.

"I honestly have no criticisms about my induction year! My experience has been very good and my school has supported me thoroughly whilst giving me the opportunity to experiment and learn things for myself.

"The mentoring and support has been fantastic and I really value the different courses that I am being sent on to develop me further. The induction period enables growth and provides support without adding any extra pressure to what can already be a challenging year."

PART 4
Career development

12

Continuing professional development

If you train to be a teacher you may wonder why, after having spent three years earning a degree, probably with a good classification, then working through an intensive period of training to gain QTS, you can't rest on your laurels for a while and think, "That's enough education and training for a while – now I just want to work as a teacher and earn some money."

It's a tempting thought, but the fact is you are entering a profession, and in professions the expectation is that you will continue to learn and develop throughout your career. It's what professional people do.

Why?

The willingness and commitment of people to engage in CPD throughout their career is an important characteristic of their membership of an established profession. It is something that not only will you want to do, it will motivate and inspire you. You will want to learn as much as teach. You will also be expected by others to do it and you will expect it of yourself.

Who expects me to do CPD?

Well, first of all, the public does. We all, as members of the public, expect our professional groups to stay on top of their game in our best interests. If we are relying on the expertise of doctors, nurses, lawyers, accountants and others who make important decisions on our behalf, we want them to be well trained and well informed, knowledgeable and capable to the best of their ability. We want them to be at the forefront of research and best practice in their area. It's part of why we have confidence in them and trust them to do their jobs well. The public – in particular parents, students and children in this case – want to know that the teachers teaching their children are trying to keep up with best practice on their behalf.

Imagine for a minute going to another professional, such as your doctor, and discovering that he or she had not been on any courses for the last five or 10 years or hadn't read a medical journal in that time. We would be shocked and, perhaps, ready to report them to the General Medical Council. So the public, first of all, have a legitimate expectation on you as a professional.

Second, your colleagues will expect you to commit to CPD. While teaching is a very supportive and collegial profession, it is also one that has a very low tolerance of laziness and of those who don't pull their weight. Your colleagues will want to know that you are committed to best practice too; that you are informed by research and a body of knowledge. Your colleagues will rightly become intolerant of you if you neglect your duty to do your best.

While you will soon observe and experience a wide variety of styles, preferences and traditions in teaching, with some of your colleagues wedded to methods they learned decades ago, you will not lose respect for those who are trying their best in the interests of the children.

However, you will soon lose respect for those who stop caring and who under-perform or become incompetent through a wilful lack of commitment. Such teachers are quickly marginalised in schools. The stakes are too high to carry slackers. Wilfully poor performance and incompetence has implications wider than loss of reputation for the individual concerned. Tolerating it has implications for the reputation of all teachers, as well as the school and the profession as a whole.

Third, your employers and the management of the school have a right to expect that you will engage in training and development that addresses the needs of the institution. Maintained schools are, after all, publicly funded by the tax payer. There is a huge public interest in maintaining their high standards and good quality. School management – in the shape of head teachers and senior staff – is responsible for maintaining quality. Management allocates a certain amount of the school's resources to investing in the learning and development of its staff to deliver good-quality results. Your co-operation and engagement in that process is not only desirable, it's a legitimate expectation of those who employ you.

Fourth and finally: *you.*

CPD is something you will want to engage in. You will want to learn new things as much as teach. It is motivating, inspiring and satisfying, and you will want to commit to it both for the reasons discussed above but also because it will be part of the way you plan your career development, with ambition to progress and be promoted, to greater seniority and responsibility and to fulfil your potential. CPD can be satisfying fun too; although not always . . .

Not all CPD is good CPD, especially if it's tokenistic and done as a tick-box measure to satisfy the seemingly arbitrary demands of accountability, and some professional groups openly acknowledge this. Lawyers and dentists, for example, must submit an audit of their completed professional development activity over a given period of time in order to maintain their registration to practice. Is CPD that is imposed on you, whether you choose or need to do it or not, the best way of maintaining professional standards?

CPD is one those things that clearly marks a categorical difference between being a member of a profession and being employed in a job. In most jobs, few of the expectations discussed above will apply. In a profession such as teaching, they all do.

What is CPD?

CPD can take a variety of forms. It can be focused on you and your needs and ambitions as an individual, on the collective needs of your colleagues as fellow professionals, and on the school as a public service institution. It can be quite specific and tactical – for example, you may need ideas to help a particular child with specific strategies to improve their reading. Or, the CPD can be general and strategic – for example, you may want to research social and collaborative learning strategies for an MA, or be working as part of a cross-departmental effort to improve pupil attendance at your school.

School-based CPD

Particularly as a new teacher, much of the professional development you will be engaged with is based in school. Some of it will enable you to be better informed and keep up with government policies and changes to things such as the National Curriculum, the exam system or national strategies in literacy or numeracy. At other times, it might involve preparing for an Ofsted inspection, bringing in outside expertise to run a training session, or even a whole day spent on some focal point of the school development plan such as the teaching of literacy across a Key Stage, improving pupil behaviour or addressing the under-achievement of particular groups of children.

Other in-school CPD might use the expertise of staff within the school, such as drawing on the knowledge, monitoring and analysis of the special needs co-ordinator (SENCO) to improve the attainment and integration of pupils with special needs.

CPD sessions often take place during the five INSET days allocated to the timetable of the school year. However, many schools will regularly use staff meetings or departmental meetings for staff and professional development opportunities. Some of these – perhaps the more informal ones where you and your colleagues plan and deliver the sessions – can often be the most valuable and effective.

For example, research into CPD in recent years has shown that some of the most effective – in terms of the impact on teachers' effectiveness and pupils' attainment – is that which is organised on an almost ad hoc basis by teachers working alongside each other in relatively informal but collaborative and co-operative ways in their own schools.

In these examples, you might find teachers working together on small action-research projects to improve the attainment of boys' writing in Years 5 and 6 in a large primary school, or a group of teachers coming together to look at effective methods of teaching various aspects of maths A level.

Nowadays, it is not uncommon for this kind of collaboration to take place between neighbouring or partner schools within the locality. Many schools have responded to local and national initiatives in recent years by coming together and using the expertise and resources of their own staff to develop from within. Both research and anecdotal evidence suggests that teachers respond better to this kind of CPD because it is directly relevant to the problems and issues they face on a daily basis. They can study the theoretical issues of pupil attainment, for example, alongside the knowledge and information they have about the real-life pupils in their own classes whose attainment they are directly involved in trying to improve. This can be highly motivating for the teachers involved because the impact can be targeted, direct and immediate.

Teachers may return to class to try out some new ideas and can see the results almost immediately. If such collaboration and co-operation is supported and regularised in a well-managed school or group of schools, then teachers not only feel well supported individually, it also does a world of good to the *esprit de corps* of the schools involved, which is very valuable in a collegial profession that relies heavily on professional peer support. Not only that, it is motivating and inspiring for you as a teacher to see the benefits you can bring to your pupils and students by learning and developing yourself through collaboration with colleagues.

However, while this kind of CPD is becoming much more common across the country, don't imagine that it is established everywhere. You may find yourself in a school where the CPD is focused very much on the school's immediate priorities of addressing the action plans from a recent Ofsted inspection, or improving pupil behaviour through top-down implementation of policies drawn up by the school's management.

The other thing that you may find is that the quality of the knowledge and skills on offer within your immediate circle of colleagues is not good enough to effect change or create sufficient impact. This may be both frustrating and de-motivating. The last thing you will want to do as a hard-pressed teacher is waste your time working with colleagues, especially after a long day, who are not putting as much time as you into a project that may require observing, researching, monitoring and assessing pupils. Effecting change and improvement is hard enough as it is without having to work with others less motivated than you.

Leadership is therefore a crucial factor in the design and delivery of CPD in a school and this is recognised by head teachers to the extent that almost all schools these days will have a designated member of staff responsible for the whole school's professional development. The development needs of individual staff will therefore be taken in to account in things such as annual appraisal meetings, where you will be able to indicate your own priorities for development.

As a new teacher, you will be very focused on the priorities set out in your induction programme and your Career Entry and Development Profile (CEDP), but as a more experienced teacher, you may want to consider opportunities to gain new qualifications, such as master's degrees or even doctoral research.

What is a CEDP?

You may not have to complete one of these as there is no longer a formal requirement to do them, but as part of your induction year you will be encouraged to reflect formally on your experience and development as a teacher through a Career Entry and Development Profile.

It is not a formal, assessed or examined part of your induction programme and is only for the benefit of yourself as an NQT. But it a structured record of your first year in teaching intended to organise the discussions and reviews you will have with your induction mentor.

The structure is loose but is linked to three transition stages:

1. the first will be initiated by your ITT tutor as you graduate your training

2. the second is at the beginning of the induction year

3. the third is as the year comes to a close and will be with you induction tutor.

The profile focuses on themes and issues such as:

- your own early development priorities and needs

- setting objectives and constructing action plans for your development

- reflections and records of transition points throughout the year.

CPD beyond school

Many teachers will prefer to focus their learning and development on more formal courses and activities that take them away from their school setting — at universities, colleges or teacher development centres run and managed by local authorities (where these centres still exist). This may be because they find it more stimulating, challenging and structured. It's also quite nice to leave the immediate pressures, concerns and the environment of the school behind and distract yourself with a course, especially where it provides some "brain food" that is relevant, interesting and useful to your practice.

Local authority professional development centres

There are still some local authorities that maintain courses and programmes of professional development for teachers hosted by local professional development centres. The most likely ones will be your induction programme.

In recent years, this provision has been undermined by the fact that many schools no longer have a close relationship with their local authority — having adopted academy status, for example — and have invested their funds for professional development into courses and programmes that they can determine more directly according to their school needs.

Nevertheless, some local authorities still host a range of courses for teachers that cover a variety of subject or phase issues and where teachers can gather and network. Such courses are often advertised through brochures or leaflets in the staff room. If you see courses that you think are relevant and useful, you can ask your head teacher or designated CPD co-ordinator whether you can attend; particularly if it is a subject or area that you have agreed is a priority for you in your induction programme or review meetings. Although you may find, even if it is an identified need, the school CPD budget has been spent!

Master's degrees

In recent decades, master's degrees have become an extremely popular vehicle for teachers' professional development, particularly where universities have linked them in part to the acquisition of other professional qualifications such as the PGCE, made them sufficiently flexible to allow study over a number of years, and included reflections on practical school experience as a large element in the design of the degree.

If you decide to train to be a teacher at a university via either undergraduate or postgraduate routes, you will almost certainly find that by the end of the course, the university is offering you a pathway to acquire a master's degree. They will almost certainly give you incentives to take it too, either by offering discounted fees for part of it, or allowing you some credits towards it on condition of meeting certain standards at the point of graduation from your training course.

Some government policies in recent years have supported moves to promote teaching as a master's-level profession, although that seems highly unlikely to take hold in the UK in the way it has in places such as the USA.

Master's degrees can still be a very attractive option for a teacher wanting to continue:

- to develop their passion for their subject or a specialist interest

- high-level professional development within a structured and academic environment

- to gain educational qualifications to add to their professional CV

- to meet, discuss and network with other highly engaged professionals, particularly those with an academic interest in education and teaching.

But be careful. Master's degrees are also:

- expensive, and the days when a school or local authority will pay the fees for you to do one are long gone

- time-consuming and demanding, both intellectually and emotionally (and if you are thinking about a PhD, multiply those demands tenfold!)

- not a direct route to promotion or seniority – don't think having the letters MA after your name improves your chances of advancement in teaching, as competence and experience always trump qualifications once you have entered the profession.

Subject associations

Many teachers will join a subject association, such as the National Association of the Teaching of English or the Mathematical Association among many others, to gain access to a wider network of support and advice, and help their professional development. Such associations will have websites with discussion forums, online communities, publications, newsletters and even conferences that help teachers to learn and develop their interests with others passionate about their subject.

They are not very expensive to join and will connect you to other subject-specialist professionals, from right across the country and even abroad. Apart from helping you to develop professionally, they will enable you to engage in wider policy debates about the future of the subject and perhaps influence government policy.

Professional associations and unions

Teachers, unions will have a similar array of services and platforms for professional development, and these are often well resourced. For example, unions will invest in areas of concern for their members. such as positive pupil behaviour strategies, plus a wide range of discussion forums and online communities addressing various subjects, phases and issues. Unions produce regular, good-quality publications, policy documents and newsletters. Their annual conferences will also include opportunities to engage in a range of education policy debates, as well as workshops on a variety of teaching topics. Some unions, particularly the NUT, will promote themselves not just as a traditional union campaigning on issues of pay and conditions, but also as a professional association, with a wider agenda of interests and concerns.

As a new teacher, CPD will be an important feature of your early development and support. Try to make sure that you don't lose focus on that among all the other things you have to cope with, especially in your induction year, when you will have an entitlement to a programme of funded support. Don't waste the opportunities that the year provides, because in future, really good CPD opportunities may feel more like a privilege than an entitlement.

Don't think that CPD is all down to your employer to fund and provide. Invest in yourself from time to time. You're worth it!

Reflections from the newteachersblogger – newteachersblog.wordpress.com

CPD: Whose responsibility is it?

Professionals recognise that they have a responsibility to maintain and develop their skills, knowledge and the quality of their professional practice.

But whose responsibility is it to do that?

Is it the responsibility of the professional individual: the doctor, dentist, lawyer, accountant, nurse or teacher?

Is it the responsibility of professional bodies charged with regulating the competence and conduct of a profession through codes of practice: the General Medical Council, the Nursing and Midwifery Council, the Bar Council?

Is it the responsibility of employers trying to provide high standards of service to the public?

One evening, I was at a private social function and an acquaintance – a dentist who lived nearby – and I started discussing professionalism in our respective domains. He questioned whether teaching can really be counted as a profession if CPD is not a formal requirement linked to obligatory registration status, as it is in dentistry.

He described to me how as a dentist he has to regularly submit evidence of CPD as a necessary requirement of maintaining his registration status with his professional body, the General Dental Council. He described how there is a similar requirement for nurses, lawyers and many others. It was an interesting discussion and it made me reflect.

Teaching no longer has a professional body – the General Teaching Council was abolished by the government in 2012. Does that weaken the credentials for teaching as a profession?

It also made me reflect on an incident that took place while I was a head teacher.

I had three excellent senior teachers who wanted to become deputy heads. They asked me if they could they attend deputy headship training. I agreed and said that although the suggestion had come from them, I would be willing to fund 50% of the cost from school CPD funds if they were happy to pay the rest. I was a more than a little dismayed when all three expressed both surprise and disappointment at the suggestion. They said they expected the school to pay the full cost.

I was offering to part-fund training that would not only take them out of school for regular and considerable periods of time but probably – almost certainly – ultimately enable their promotion from and permanent loss to the school.

As a teacher, I wanted to develop the expertise of my fellow professionals. I also wanted to develop them all as assets to the profession. But as an employer-manager, I also had a responsibility to balance the needs of the school with the ambitions of those employed by it.

13

Moving on and up

As a new teacher, you will be focusing on making sure that you get through your induction year successfully. But as it draws to a close, and especially once you have got it out of the way, you will reflect more and more on where to go from here. Unless you have had a bad experience and been poorly supported, or some particular personal circumstances deem it necessary, you will almost certainly want to stay at least another year in the same school.

There's a very good reason for this — consolidation. Teaching is very demanding and challenging in terms of the level of competence you must exercise daily and the quality of the relationships you need to establish just to function. Once you have got some of those patterns and behaviours established, you won't want to give them up very quickly to have to start all over again somewhere else. So a very good reason to stay put will be your own need for consolidation, reinforcement and affirmation.

Besides, the children and students need consistency and stability in order to learn. Coping with change is part of life and we all have to deal with it, but too much change can be very damaging, especially in the relationship between teacher and student.

Most teachers would advise that, unless there are compelling reasons to do so, stay at least one more year to consolidate all that you have learned before thinking of a move.

However, your first year might have been a negative and dispiriting experience where you felt unsupported and unrecognised. You may have even been unhappy. You may have concluded that you can't stand another day in the presence of your miserable colleagues and awful kids and it's just best to cut your losses and move on. It happens.

Whatever your experience in the first year or so, at some point it will occur to you to make a move of some sort.

Teaching is a career where you can make rapid progress both in terms of responsibility, management and seniority. While it's not generally thought of as highly paid, at least compared to some professions, its ranking in the pay league has improved significantly in the last decade.

Entry-level pay for example, compares well even with most other established professions, particularly if you are a recent graduate with a good degree in a shortage subject where there will be additional incentives to recruit you. The opportunities for mobility are excellent too, and although the number of teaching vacancies can vary enormously from one region to another, given that there are well over 30,000 schools in the UK employing over 600,000 teachers, you have a better chance of moving around the country and still finding employment as a teacher than you do a position in most other professions.

But where teaching really stands out is the opportunities it offers for people who want to take on management and responsibility. An ambitious person who is focused on developing management and leadership as well as teaching skills can progress rapidly up the promotion and pay ladder.

All of these factors mean that within a relatively short period of starting your first job in a school, you can if you want start thinking about whether moving onwards and upwards is a realistic option.

Of course, the motives behind a desire to progress can be a very subjective and personal. If you teach in a school where you are very happy and feel challenged and stimulated just by what teaching throws at you every day, then like many teachers you may find that the last thing you want to do is give yourself a headache taking on the co-ordination of a curriculum area, running a department and managing other staff. Moving on up doesn't necessarily mean moving elsewhere.

Changing roles

You do not need to win a formal pay-related promotion to take on more responsibility in a school. Indeed, in many schools, both primary and secondary, the school managers will, if they are any good, look to offer you positions of additional responsibility as soon as your induction year is out of the way, as a way of developing you. This may be doing things such as running the under-14 football team, getting involved in extra-curricular activities such as the school orchestra or the athletics club or, in a primary school in particular, co-ordinating a relatively minor curriculum area such as art and craft or dance and drama.

Be careful, though, that your competence and willingness is not easily exploited. Teachers are generally very hard-working people who want to do as much as possible for schools whose finances are perennially strapped. Make sure that you are not doing something for free that others were previously paid for, or that you find yourself taking on more and more each year with little or no additional remuneration.

However, you may find that your first opportunity for advancement comes at the school where you started your first appointment. While fair employment and equal opportunities procedures exist for a good reason, you will usually have the advantage of knowing earlier than anyone outside the school that a colleague is thinking of leaving, planning to retire or take maternity leave, and that their job is about to be advertised. You can at least start thinking about whether the post and timing is right for you, if not planning and preparing your strategy.

Job titles can be very misleading in schools and may be almost meaningless out of context. Being head of IT in a small primary is not the same thing as being head of IT in a large secondary school specialising in technology. Being a deputy head teacher in a large secondary school may mean you are one of number who hold the title and where your responsibilities are quite narrow and specialised. If you are deputy head in a primary school, you may be running a couple of important curriculum areas and be responsible for assessment, record-keeping and pastoral care across the entire school.

In secondary schools, the path to additional responsibility has two strands. One focuses more on the pastoral care of students, where you might become head of year and go on to be assistant head teacher. The other concentrates more on curriculum responsibility and development, where you might first become a Key Stage co-ordinator for English, for example, then deputy or head of department. In primary schools, these strands tend to overlap with each other much more.

One of those most important considerations for you making your first move into management, even if it is only the lower echelons, is the change of role that you will have to cope with. For the first time, you may be managing other adults. Teachers are usually extremely effective at managing children and young people – they plan and prepare for them, direct and organise their movements and activity, and motivate, enthuse and inspire them. In short, they provide leadership for them. When it comes to doing that with adults for the first time, some people completely lose the plot, forgetting that the principles are the same even if they have to be applied with a slightly different tone of voice.

As a manager, either of a department or curriculum area, you are no longer one of the boys or girls in quite the same way. You will have to put a little distance and formality into some aspects of your working relationship with the colleagues you sit next to in the staff room and may socialise with at weekends, at least while you are in school and in that role. In a highly collegial profession such as teaching, changing roles and personas with colleagues comes as one of the most complex of challenges.

These are not necessarily different to the challenges you will face in any job or profession where you have to manage other people or where there is a target-driven culture that pressures working relationships, but the highly collegial nature of teaching adds complexity.

Nevertheless, taking on a promotion has positive and satisfying challenges associated with it as well, and if you have chosen your new post well, you will soon feel the exhilaration of your competence being stretched to its full potential or having achieved something difficult under pressure.

As we have said, teaching is, generally speaking, a very supportive profession with a very strong team ethic, mutual respect for fellow professionals and often infused with deep personal relationships and lifelong friendships. Because of this, the more aggressive and competitive aspects of getting on and promotion are often absent; at least, compared to environments in some commercial and industrial sectors. Teaching is not the kind of environment where, by and large, you will feel you have missed the boat if you are not in a certain position by a certain age.

While you will meet the occasional go-getting 25-year-old head teacher of a primary school who has been fast-tracked and groomed, you will also meet the 55-year-old recently appointed deputy heads who have taken the tortoise's route to senior management rather than the hare's. The imperative to be ambitious and competitive, while it exists in teaching, is more often than not tempered by the moral and social purpose of the profession.

Which is perhaps all the more reason why you should ask yourself these two questions when you think of moving onwards and upwards as a teacher: why, and why not?

Thinking about why

- What kind of teacher am I? Do I want to make the most difference I can, gradually working in the most challenging schools with the most challenging children?

- Am I looking to extend and broaden my experience as a teacher, perhaps gaining new skills as part of acquiring greater expertise?

- Am I seeking to challenge myself in untried and untested areas of my career?

- Have I become a little stale and entrenched in some teaching routines, and do I need to make a change?

- Have I mapped out, or even sketched out, an ideal career plan, with job titles and dates for achieving them?

- Do I need to work with new people and experience a greater variety of teaching methods, techniques and philosophies?

- Do I want to earn more money – for myself or for my family?

- Do I want to challenge myself personally in management and leadership roles with considerable complexity and responsibility?

- Do I want to change my environment – a new school, a new town, a new part of the country?

- Do I find pressure and stress invigorating?

Thinking about why not

- What kind of teacher am I? Do I want to focus on developing my craft and my subject knowledge to the highest level?

- Do I dislike change – do I *really* want to accommodate new school routines, systems, policies and rules?

- Do I like where I live – would moving affect the way I relate to my friends, neighbours, the town, the area?

- Do I want to put in the effort of establishing my authority and my teaching reputation all over again?

- Do I enjoy the stress that comes with forging new relationships and trying to motivate and inspire people I don't know?

- Do I like being the outsider or the new person?

- Do I find pressure and stress debilitating?

Stress

There are many rewards to being promoted, of course, but there is one thing that is almost certainly associated with taking additional responsibility in a management and leadership position in teaching, and that is stress.

Teaching is not always stressful, but when stress comes it doesn't always know when to stop. The more responsibility you have, the more likely you will have to cope with the associated stress.

As a class teacher, even with no additional responsibility, you will have the daily stresses of planning and preparing sufficiently not to feel panicky. Then there's managing the children — even if they're not a particularly challenging bunch. There will be times when you are not in the mood for the smart alecs and the petty disruptions. Then there's the marking, assessment records, profiles and paperwork you have to keep on top of, plus the staff meetings, phase or departmental meetings . . .

Now, with your promotion, you have to do all of these things, plus:

- supporting and mentoring new colleagues

- dealing with the more serious behaviour issues of very challenging children

- dealing with parental complaints

- managing the performance of colleagues less effective and motivated than you

- chasing colleagues to complete tasks they haven't done yet, such as overdue planning, assessments and reports

- chairing meetings with colleagues who look tired and sound bored

- attend governors meetings where they ask demanding questions . . .

All this while you are still:

- chasing externally imposed, challenging and even unrealistic targets

- trying to improve on last year's test and exam results

- preparing for an imminent Ofsted inspection.

Are you sure you still want that promotion?

Schools are communities with distinct cultures

When you do decide to take that leap and apply for a new job elsewhere, you'll be surprised how different schools can be from each other. All workplaces have an atmosphere or a culture that either seems friendly or stand-offish, relaxed or business-like, lackadaisical or focused. Schools are no different in that respect, but they are operating as communities in a way that few other organisations, even in the public sector let alone the private, have to operate.

When going for a job in a school at any point in your career, bear in mind the cultural aspects of the organisation you applying to join.

- What are the head teacher and the senior management team like? Do they appear:

  ○ approachable, supportive, open to suggestions and new ideas?

  ○ bureaucratic, officious and business-like? Are they in their offices most of the time or are they seen in the staff room and in classrooms, communicating and relating to colleagues and students?

- What are your colleagues like? Do they seem:

  ○ to get on well with each other, chat, laugh, have fun, or do they appear cynical, disillusioned, negative?

  ○ to collaborate, co-operate, have and share ideas and respect each other's professionalism?

- What are the children and students like?

  ○ Do they show respect for each other, the teachers and support staff and the school building and environment?

  ○ Depending on where you live and what kind of school you want to teach in, are they a good mix in terms of their social, ethnic, cultural background?

These are important questions for you to keep in mind, alongside the reasons why moving on and up have come to the fore. Being ambitious is as laudable in teaching as it is in any other profession where the quality of leadership is so crucial. Just bear in mind the values and the culture of teaching and of schools as you make your way up the greasy pole. Doing so will help you make the most of your ambition.

Reflections from the newteachersblogger – newteachersblog.wordpress.com

Manage your privacy

As a teacher, you'll need to manage your privacy, perhaps more than most people.

But be careful of those who try to "manage" it for you.

I recently learned of a school whose contract stipulated that teachers employed there must agree not to use Facebook. This wasn't advice. This was in the contract. I've also read reports of head teachers running job applicants through Google to see what their online profile looks like.

This seems to me to be an intrusion into personal privacy.

In my view, any responsible employee, professional or otherwise, should agree to refrain from actions that might wilfully bring their employers into disrepute. This is especially true in teaching. We should have a responsibility not just for our own reputation but also for the reputation of our school and, indeed, our profession.

But is what we do in our personal and private lives really the business of anyone else? As long as it's legal, of course.

A new teacher said to me recently: "Yes, but putting your photos on Facebook, getting drunk or going naked in Ibiza might be personal. But it's no longer private if you've put them on the internet!"

Of course, we should manage our reputations cautiously. But why shouldn't we share our silly photos, however embarrassing they may be, with our friends, even on Facebook? It is, after all, a social network for you and your friends. It's not intended for the whole world, even if it has the power to search it.

We must manage this. We must make it clear to our friends that they may be compromising us by doing something like that. If not, we may need to re-evaluate who our friends are. Friends sharing our embarrassing pictures on the internet is no different (in principle) to friends sharing our personal photos, gossip or private letters in a pub or club with people we don't know or trust. We soon stop being friends with people whose discretion we can't rely on.

In my view, employers should not be googling us or checking our Facebook profiles to inform their judgement about us as teachers, any more than they should be contacting our friends for a reference about how we behave in pubs or clubs on a Saturday night. Making a judgement about our personal and private lives is not a professional judgement; it's a moral one.

Not all of our personal life can be private. Nor should it be. Much of our personal and private life is lived out in the public sphere. Having a private, personal conversation with a close friend in a coffee shop doesn't mean that it's a public conversation.

As new teachers, we should know not to recklessly put our own, or the school's, reputation in jeopardy. But parents, students and especially employers should know when not to intrude into our personal privacy. And if they don't, it's part of our responsibility to tell them.

14

Alternatives to teaching

After a year or two in teaching, it may be the case that one of the options you have considered, alongside moving on and up, is moving out.

Many professions have high churn rates, and teaching is no exception. Recent research indicated that within five years of entering teaching, up to 25% of teachers were leaving. Some would do so temporarily of course, perhaps to have children. Others indicated that they felt overwhelmed by the responsibility, the workload, the lack of work–life balance, the unreasonable levels of expectation.

Other research done by the now-defunct General Teaching Council for England revealed a surprising number of people who completed a teacher-training course but did not enter the profession. Of an annual cohort of 25,000–30,000 new teachers, 10%–20% would not take up an immediate first appointment. Sometimes, this would represent people taking a year out to travel or start a family; others simply decided that although they would finish the course and get a qualification, teaching as a career was not for them.

With such a substantial number leaving or not entering the profession in the first place, it would be wise to consider what alternative options you might have, were you to train as a teacher but decide the life of Mr Chips was not going to be your vocation.

Fortunately, there are quite a lot of options, both on the fringes of teaching and as far away as you can get from it!

Supply teaching

Few, if any, people go in to teaching to be supply teachers. But a lot of new teachers, unable to find a permanent job, take short- and even long-term supply assignments until a better option comes along. Indeed, if you are any good, you won't be on supply too long, because the schools you work at will spot you as a talent and find a way of offering you a permanent job.

There are even some who have found it an agreeable long-term alternative to a permanent position in teaching, perhaps because of family or other responsibilities, or because they simply prefer the flexibility it offers.

The advantages of supply teaching are that it is quite well paid as a daily rate, and that you don't have to do a lot of the paperwork, planning, marking, meetings, extra-curricular activities and so on that permanent teachers do – at least, if you are on short-term assignments, although you would be expected to do some of this if you were engaged for a few weeks or months continuously. You also get to see a wide variety of schools and children, and if you don't like them, you'll have the pleasure of telling them you don't want to work there any more.

On the other hand, the work is increasingly irregular since new cover arrangements have come in that allow TAs to take classes for limited periods. It's also usually a much harder job. You won't know your way around the school or get access to resources easily. It's more difficult to establish relationships with children and discipline them when they know they can try it on with you. Other teachers won't have the same regard for you either – you won't usually feel part of the team, and you almost certainly won't get holiday or sick pay unless you can negotiate it as part of a really long-term assignment.

Teaching abroad

The huge asset that you have as a qualified teacher trained in the UK is that you are a member of a profession that is in demand worldwide. English is usually the lingua franca of many international schools. Teaching abroad offers many opportunities and advantages for those seeking to live and work in a different part of the world with easy access to different people, languages and cultures, and the possibility of travel and adventure.

These days, there is a global market for teachers. You are just as likely to have colleagues who hail from Australia, New Zealand, North America, South Africa and other major Commonwealth countries as you are from other parts of the UK, especially in large cities. That flow is reciprocal, and as a UK-trained, native English-speaking, qualified teacher, you would be an attractive prospect across the world. In some places, such as Australia and New Zealand, demand has been quite acute at times.

Teaching in developed countries with educational systems similar to our own is a relatively easy transition. Many teachers who have gone to Australia, for example, find issues such as workload, pupil behaviour and accountability are remarkably similar to those they left behind in the UK. However, the different climate, and we're talking meteorology here, can have a remarkable effect on general outlook and perception!

There are also many opportunities for teaching in a voluntary capacity, either for small charities working in developing countries or directly with organisations that manage larger education and teaching projects such as Voluntary Service Overseas (www.vso.org.uk). There is competition for such positions, and a minimum time commitment of not less than two years.

A growing network of international schools can be found right across the world as well. They are international in that they cater largely for the children of expatriate commercial and industrial employees, and sometimes wealthy local residents wanting their children educated in the English language. The educational culture of international schools is of course very different to that you would find in the UK, and even quite distinct from that of the UK's independent sector.

For one thing, the curriculum and syllabus is perhaps more likely to be that of the International Baccalaureate (IB), except where a given location is totally dominated by British expatriates. But one of the many attractions of teaching in international schools is that, although there will be an expectation to commit to high levels of extra-curricular activity, there may be much greater emphasis on a broader, balanced and more rounded education. This, coupled with the generally much lighter emphasis on regular formal assessments typical in UK schooling, can make teaching very enjoyable.

The difficulty for those who have spent a good deal of time teaching abroad is that they often find it very difficult to re-integrate into the UK system, should they choose to return. On their return, many perceive the pace and extent of change in the UK education system as too difficult to accommodate.

However, the reality is that many of the changes are relatively superficial and cosmetic. Teaching as a discipline and schools as institutions change little over time. Schools, particularly those in developed countries, are in essence organised more or less the way they were a hundred years ago. The core curriculum is still largely unchanged, even where schools are very innovative with new technology.

The internet also provides easy, instant access to UK education news, policies and resources, so international school teachers are not out of touch at all. Nevertheless, the perception of difference is still there. It also runs both ways. Sometimes, returning teachers are overlooked as serious candidates, particularly at senior management level, because school governors perceive them to be out of touch with the latest changes or innovations. While teaching abroad in the international school sector has enormous benefits, if you plan to return to the UK then make sure you plan your re-entry strategy from an early stage.

Teaching assistant

A few years ago, analysis of the register of the General Teaching Council for England found many thousands of qualified teachers who were working full-time in schools, but not as teachers; rather, as TAs. Anecdotal evidence suggested that the reasons they had chosen to do this was that, while still wanting to work with children and in an educational environment, they simply did not want the weighty and complex responsibilities that came with a full-time teacher position, particularly the workload.

The number of TAs in schools across the UK has expanded enormously in recent years, to the extent that some schools employ a TA in every classroom, and they can be found not only teaching small groups of children and students, but sometimes covering whole classes for limited periods; although this is normally done under the direction of a qualified teacher. Training has also improved and formalised to meet the growing demands of the role, so there are now even higher-level TAs who have taken on specialist roles with additional pay. Many are employed purely to support the teaching of mathematics or special needs.

The crucial difference, of course, is responsibility. While teachers will still have the onerous responsibilities of planning, preparing, marking, assessing, recording, reporting, attending meetings and organising extra-curricular activities, TAs do not. For some, the additional pay and status of being a teacher is not adequate compensation for the impact the workload and responsibility have on lifestyle.

Other roles in schools

Similarly, if you love working with young people and want to be involved in education but don't want to be a classroom teacher, there are opportunities in other roles. For example, if you were passionate about literature and books but discovered that teaching wasn't for you, your teaching qualifications and skills would stand you in good stead if you wanted to work as a school librarian. Librarianship is a distinct profession, of course, and requires additional qualifications, but it is easy to see how that move can be made in a relatively short step if you are motivated to take it.

In the same way, many teachers have found themselves to be fascinated by educational psychology or child development. Many educational psychologists started life as teachers, and have acquired additional qualifications to enable them to move into that field. Doing so satisfies the needs of those who would still like regular access to working with children while pursuing their interest and ambitions in applied psychology or child development.

In recent years, there has been an increasing number of opportunities for specialist teachers to be employed in peripatetic roles too – where they work part time in a number of schools providing a specialist service. The government has funded a number of initiatives in recent years, particularly in promoting instrumental music tuition, singing in choirs, the teaching of MFLs in primary schools, and a variety of sports and PE provision. These opportunities are not commonplace or universally available and funding is variably allocated, but they do exist in greater numbers and do provide options for qualified teachers with suitable skills and specialist knowledge who want to remain in teaching but without the associated baggage that most classroom teachers have to bear.

Tutoring

Private tutoring can be an alternative to teaching for those highly qualified in specialist skills, subjects or areas that are in high demand. For example, if you are a qualified teacher and can teach piano to Grade 8, or if you are a physics teacher and can teach to A level, you may find that the demand for your knowledge and skills makes tutoring a viable financial alternative to mainstream teaching.

Depending on the market in the area where you live, there may be sufficient demand for tutoring from parents who want their children to have regular additional support for maths and English in Year 6 SATs, or for entry exams to selective schools, for example. It is unlikely, however, that you would be able to rely on tutoring alone as an alternative career unless there is the prospect of becoming well established with an excellent reputation in an area with high regular demand for your particular skills and specialism.

Transferable skills for commerce and industry

There is no doubt that teaching fosters some excellent and highly sought-after skills in a very wide range of other sectors of the economy. As we discussed at the beginning of the book and elsewhere, good teachers:

- **are excellent communicators**

- are highly organised

- are good planners

- have strategic vision

- implement complex tasks in structured and methodical ways

- can motivate and inspire difficult, challenging and de-motivated people

- can work collaboratively and co-operatively in teams

- can work to produce high-quality outcomes under extreme pressure

- are diligent, conscientious and hard-working.

With a CV that includes these skills and attributes, even Lord Sugar would look at you and say "You're hired!"

The problem is that most teachers don't look at themselves like that. Take most teachers out of the context of a school and they either lose the confidence to transfer those skills or they simply don't recognise them as skills of the same value.

Those with the confidence to identify and transfer their teaching skills can reap rich rewards. Just take the creative industries, in which the UK is a world leader, as an example. Look up the background of some of our most talented and successful artists, whether visual, musical, dramatic, literary, and see how many of them started their careers in teaching: people such as D. H. Lawrence, George Orwell, John Fowles, Dawn French, J.K. Rowling and Sting. More examples abound.

Apart from those with high profiles, there are literally thousands of other roles in the creative industries that lend themselves to the skills teachers develop and acquire: for instance, producers, directors, technicians, writers, editors. Of course, if you moved from teaching into these sectors you would almost certainly have to start at the bottom of the ladder. But you wouldn't have to master a whole new skill set.

Three other areas in which the UK is a world leader are the burgeoning web development, coding, gaming and information technology industries; the perennially lucrative pharmaceutical industry; and Britain's seemingly bottomless gold-mine of tourism. One of the key reasons that people are attracted to teaching in the first place is the love of their subject. That is also one of the reasons that people leave teaching, too, particularly if a passion for research or development in their sector is not satisfied by a life in the classroom. The attractions of industry can be difficult to resist, particularly if that industry is buoyant or booming and there is an opportunity to follow a specialist passion to a very high level at a salary commensurate with expertise.

The "soft skills" that teaching fosters so well, such as communication and interpersonal skills, are in high demand in the tourist industry. People who can transfer these skills from children to adults are highly marketable. Teachers can also, therefore, find it very easy to move into jobs and professions that depend on coaching, training, counselling or personnel management, such as sports coaches and instructors, industrial and commercial skills trainers or social workers.

In short, there is a wide world out there to which teachers can apply their skills, knowledge and aptitudes — if they have the confidence to project themselves on to it. Perhaps it's just as well they don't, or we would have another crisis in teacher retention!

Conclusion

If you have reached this far in the book and still have an open mind about whether teaching is the right career for you, then don't stop now. This concluding chapter is intended to offer enough evidence to convince you – one way or the other.

Obviously, talking to people who are teachers is an important tactic in weighing up the advantages and disadvantages, the rewards and sacrifices, the pros and cons. So do it. Talk to lots of different teachers – new and experienced, young and old, men and women, primary and secondary, as many as you can. But be careful.

As in many jobs and professions that are very demanding and arguably under-appreciated, you'll come across people with a slightly cynical, jaundiced if not embittered attitude. That's not to say they are not right about their particular view; they may well be, but the circumstances they describe may be very personal to them. So if you do meet people who present a negative view and advise you to steer clear of teaching, try to find out what the particular issues were for them and how they developed over time. Was it the politics of school life or the politics of society? Was it the workload? The kids? Their own ageing process? Try to get them to reflect honestly.

Conclusion

As this book has tried to emphasise, you will need to examine yourself and your own motives honestly, even forensically, when considering teaching as a career. Your personality and character will have a huge bearing on whether you will be a good teacher or not. You will need to be robust emotionally and confident that your inner strengths are sufficient enough to cope with intense periods of hard work, pressure and even stress. You need to know that you like children and empathise with their predicament; childhood is not always a happy, care-free and innocent state. But perhaps above all, you will need to be a positive person, prepared to look adversity in the face and smile straight back.

Teaching is both physically and emotionally demanding, and the range of tasks, roles and expectations constantly seems to grow and never seems to be completed or satisfied. Your "to do" list will always be a long one. This can lead to a feeling that, however hard you work, however many extra hours you put in at weekends and in your own time, it will never be enough to feel as if you are doing the job properly, especially in the eyes of those sent in to inspect what you do at a moment's notice. That can lead to a deep cynicism, even bitterness in you and your colleagues. It may even lead to a breakdown in your health and well-being, where your sleep might be regularly disturbed, where you may suffer from bouts of depression, where the stress of even low-level but regular misbehaviour and disruption, let alone the possible threat of intimidation or violence from emotionally disturbed pupils or their parents, may send you over the edge. You may feel stuck in a rut, trapped by lack of opportunity for promotion or mobility in the area you teach. You'll often feel misrepresented, misunderstood, unappreciated and under-valued. In comparison to many other professions, you may feel as if what you do lacks sophistication, glamour and public recognition – certainly in financial terms. All of these are very real issues and concerns, and every experienced teacher reading this will instantly recognise them.

On the other hand, if you are that positive person who has the resilience to face down adversity, you will see these issues as opportunities. You will see teaching as a job that offers an endless variety of chances for interacting with the energy and vitality of children and young people, for being creative and innovative, for helping to solve personal problems and for tackling some of the most intractable social issues of our time. You will see that the job is what you want to make of it, that you are still largely your own boss, and the issues of workload, stress and complex responsibility will positively challenge and develop your management and leadership skills like few other jobs or professions can. You will do a job that is endlessly interesting, engaging and work with subjects that you love. You will *never* be bored. You will work family-friendly hours with long holidays. Your job will be secure, reasonably well paid, with automatic pay rises, has one of the best final-salary pensions in the public sector and, when you do retire, if you have had a good career, you will be lauded and remembered by generations of individuals and an appreciative local community.

But perhaps the best way to consider these issues, both pros and cons, is to listen to someone who went through this process. Laura McInerney became a teacher after careful, even analytical, consideration of the rewards and sacrifices, and she describes her view with compelling clarity.

> "Prior to teaching, I worked in a job where I sat looking at spreadsheets all day and at some point I just thought: 'If I die tomorrow, people will stand up at my funeral and they will tell the world that I spent my days looking at a computer.' That thought terrified me into quitting.

> "I wanted to become a teacher because I figured out that being able to transmit information to groups of 30 people, many of whom were not necessarily motivated to be there, sounded like a really cool skill to learn. I also wanted to develop a thicker skin, and I wanted a job that had immediacy – where there were things to do all day long and those things would have immediate feedback. What did I have to offer?

> "Resilience: the desire to really want to do a good job, make a difference, learn how to be a good teacher, and the determination to get up and do it all again tomorrow when things went disastrously wrong (which they did – a lot).

> "Concentration: mixed with an ability to laugh at myself. I'm quite difficult to embarrass or throw off course. Partly this is because when I concentrate on something it gets all of my attention, partly because if something makes me look ridiculous then I am willing to laugh at it. Many new teachers become hung-up on looking stupid in front of their class, and one of the things I learned quickly was how to laugh through that and shake it off.

Conclusion

"Prior work: I'd had several jobs, including being a floor manager in McDonalds and working as a management consultant. Although neither is directly related to being a teacher, both were quite gruelling with long hours and involved working in small teams in a high-pressure atmosphere, and those skills are quite useful for working in schools.

"Experience? I didn't have any. No younger brothers or sisters even.

"What have I learnt from teaching?

"Confidence: before I started teaching I was never very good in social situations, but once you get used to being in charge of 30 people, six times a day, then it is much easier to be confident.

"Presenting and explaining: the essence of being a good teacher is being able to explain complicated materials using the right examples and in the right order, so eventually someone else holds the materials in their own brain. Learning how to do that well is incredibly difficult, but if you can then it becomes easier to explain lots of things to people — directions to a lost tourist or a recipe to your dad over the phone, or even telling naughty kids on an aeroplane why exactly it is they need to stay in their seats!

"The pros and cons of being a teacher?

"It is shattering to be on your feet for six or seven hours, plus marking and planning. Schools are very sensory environments — they are noisy, they smell, and you can't switch them off. Once the school day starts you are 'on show' and there's no escaping until it's finished. You can't take time off to go to people's weddings (or anything else happening outside of the holidays). Young people will intentionally set out to hurt and upset you, and that can be tough to take (at least initially). No-one is naturally able to do it. You will have to work at it, continually. It's hard to do well, so there's always more to learn about and improve. But at least people know what your job is when you tell them what you do.

"Children are endlessly novel and interesting. You get to move around all day. There is a surprising amount of autonomy in lessons to try out different things and create your own materials. You get to talk about your favourite subject all day long. Supporting and mentoring other teachers as you develop is as rewarding as working with young people. Being able to tell parents at parents' evenings how brilliant their children are doing (especially if this is a new development!) Helping students with pastoral needs, for example resolving issues of bullying, and seeing their personal development afterwards. It is quite a privilege to be involved in the lives of young people and help them figure out who they are and what they are good at. The feeling that you get when a student finally grasps a really difficult concept — that above all, is priceless."

If you become a teacher, you will have the opportunity to have that feeling every day. You won't get it *every* day, mind you, but you will most days. When you see a child's face light up because they know they have learned something, you will know too that a window has been opened from their mind onto the world. That window has illuminated a potential future of possibility and achievement that they could not have envisioned without what you have just done as a teacher.

You have taught them something new. Just think of that for a moment. Just think of the legacy you could leave with hundreds, if not thousands of children and young people over the 30 or 40 years of a career in teaching, that they will remember you. They will remember you for rest of their lives for the difference you have made to them. That is a wonderful legacy to leave. That is a great job to have. So if you have what it takes, become a teacher. Good luck!

Reflections from the newteachersblogger – newteachersblog.wordpress.com

"When I retire, I want to have some memories . . . !"

So said Tim, Martin Freeman's amiable character in Ricky Gervais' *The Office*, when he told Gareth, the "assistant to the assistant manager", that he wants

Conclusion

to leave his job, go back to university and find something important to do with his life.

Teaching is very hard work, but when you do retire (and that may be a very long way off) you can look forward to memories that people such as Tim can only crave ...

In 1979 I was doing the Victorians with my class of 10-year olds. We decided to put on a Victorian Music Hall for the Christmas show. I was the Master of Ceremonies and donned a handle-bar moustache for the part. We ran the show to a packed house for three nights. Everyone laughed.

Twenty years later, I employed two young black guys who could sing and play gospel music on the piano. Within six weeks, they had trained 60 kids to sing gospel songs and to perform a concert in the local church. Their beautiful voices nearly lifted the roof off. Tears were streaming down my face.

Four years earlier, I was sitting on a tube train being stared at by a young black man in a hoodie. He got up and stood over me. "You're Mr Newland innit?" I looked up and nodded. "Darren?" "Yeah ..." he said. He sniffed. "It was good, ya kna ... !" The train stopped, the doors opened and he got off.

One day in 1986, I was teaching maths to a group of nine-year-olds struggling with long multiplication. In the middle of the session, a little boy with a speech impediment started tugging at my shirt. I turned to him. He was nodding his head. His eyes and face were beaming. "I get it now! I get it now!" he gasped with delight.

Seven years later I got an email. It read: "I've Googled Mr Newland and got this email address. Are you the Mr Newland who used to teach me between 1980–82? You were my best teacher."

Fourteen years earlier, I was in the Lake District with 30 kids doing adventure sports. One girl, who had never been out of Hackney, got lost but found her way back by asking a farmer for a lift on his tractor. Another who had never seen a horse before, was riding, fell off, but jumped straight back on it. And one boy woke me up in the middle of the night to tell me, "Sir! I've just seen the stars!"

One day in 1984, a boy with learning difficulties was painting. It was home-time, and I asked him to pack up. He said: "Can I stay here forever? I want to paint for the rest of my life!" Twenty-eight years later, he invites me to his one-man show at a gallery in west London.

Two years before that on a visit to a local museum, a girl noticed a photograph of an old railway arch that is near her house. It turned out to be the site where the first British pilot built and flew the first British aeroplane. We visited the site. It was derelict. But we campaigned to have it recognised. There's a blue plaque there now.

Five years later, an 11-year-old girl in my class refused to speak to me for three days. On Friday after school, I found a note tucked under the windscreen wiper of my car: It read: "Sorry about this week. I started. Being a woman."

Last year, the same person contacted me to say: "I've been living in Australia but I'm home to see my mum. Can we meet for coffee? I've got a little boy now and I want him to meet my teacher."

Not many jobs demand from you what teaching does. But when you retire, you'll have many more memories like this.

I promise.

Comment on this and other newteachersblogs at:

- Wordpress: newteachersblog.wordpress.com

- Twitter: @newteacherstalk

- Facebook: www.facebook.com/newteacherstalk

- LinkedIn: www.linkedin.com/groups/New-Teachers-Talk

Further resources and information

- For support, advice and information from the **Department for Education** about getting into teaching, from initial enquiry through to completion of application, write to The Teaching Line, St James House, Moon Street, Bristol, BS2 8QY, or

  o Tel: 0800 389 2500

  o Web: www.education.gov.uk/getintoteaching

  o Facebook: www.facebook.com/getintoteaching

  o YouTube: www.youtube.com/getintoteaching

  o Twitter: https://twitter.com/getintoteaching

  o blog: getintoteaching.wordpress.com

- For **live, face-to-face events**, where you can talk to advisers in person, including new teachers, visit www.education.gov.uk/teachevents.

Further resources and information

- For **specific support with applications**, take a look at www.education.gov.uk/teachtips.

- For **enquiries about the requirements and relevance of academic qualifications**, you can go to www.education.gov.uk/teachentryrequirements.

- **Premier Plus** provides personalised, one-to-one advice and support service for those with a 2.i (or have a 2.i predicted) who would like to teach at primary level, or maths, physics, chemistry, MFL, biology, history, English, geography or computer science at secondary; to find out more, visit Premier Plus at www.education.gov.uk/teachpremierplus.

- For information about **how to fund your teacher training**, see www.education.gov.uk/teachpgfunding.

- For help and advice about **getting on to a Subject Knowledge Enhancement (SKE) course** prior to starting ITT, you can have a look at www.education.gov.uk/teachske.

- For help and advice about **getting school experience** before starting an ITT course, visit www.education.gov.uk/teachsep.

- For advice and support about **passing the literacy and numeracy skills tests** prior to starting ITT, see www.education.gov.uk/teachskillstests.

- If you want to find out about applying to most undergraduate and postgraduate teacher training courses in the UK (with links to Scotland, Wales and NI), visit UCAS at www.ucas.com/how-it-all-works/teacher-training.

- **Teach First** considers applications from "exceptional graduates" – mostly those with 2.is and above from Russell Group universities – who are prepared to work in some of the most challenging schools in England, and you can find out more about the scheme at www.teachfirst.org.uk.

- **School Direct** offers information and advice on school-based teacher-training routes; visit www.education.gov.uk/teachschooldirect.

- For information and advice on **which route to take into teaching**: www.education.gov.uk/teachroutes.

Glossary

As you will have realised, teaching can be a quite jargon-heavy profession. This glossary gives a fuller explanation of some of the terms you have encountered in this book, and some more you are sure to encounter if you pursue a career in teaching.

Academy schools	schools within the maintained/state sector but which are free of local authority control and have the ability to set the terms and dates, pay and conditions of staff and some freedom around curriculum delivery; many are sponsored by businesses, charities, faith bodies and even universities
ADHD	Attention Deficit Hyperactivity Disorder: a condition that can be found in children of all intelligence variables but is characterised by a lack of focus, short attention span, fidgeting and restlessness
AfL	Assessment for Learning: a term for the kind of assessment in which teachers focus on continuous student feedback that encourages self-regulated learning

Glossary

A level	Advanced level subject exams taken towards the end of secondary school, usually at age 18 in Year 13 in England and Wales and Year 14 in Northern Ireland
AR&R	assessment, recording and reporting
ASCL	Association of School and College Leaders: a union
ATL	Association of Teachers and Lecturers: a union
Catchment area	the local area from which a school normally recruits its students, with boundaries usually determined by the local authority or school governors
Community school	a school usually funded and governed by the local authority
Core subjects	English, maths and science
CPD	continuing professional development: the learning and development that teachers will regularly engage in to keep up to date and maintain best practice, such as courses, training or additional degrees and diplomas
DfE	Department for Education
EAL	English as an additional language
EBD	Emotional and Behavioural Disorder
Ed Psych	educational psychologist
EIS	Educational Institute of Scotland: a union, affiliated to the NUT in England and Wales
ELB	Education and Library Board (Northern Ireland)
Employment-based route	teacher-training schemes that are based in schools and often salaried, such as SCITT or School Direct

ESL/ESOL	English as a Second Language/English for Speakers of Other Languages
EWO	education welfare officer: usually a local authority employee, this person works to address issues around the absence and attendance of children at school
Faith school	a school where the constitution, trust deeds or governance allows for a particular religious ethos to have a prominent role
Foundation subjects	history, geography, physical education, music, IT, PHSE, D&T, art and design
Free school	new schools, often initiated by groups of parents or charities, and entirely independent of local authorities, which can apply for direct funding from the DfE to meet a specific local need or have a particular ethos or character
GCSE	General Certificate of Secondary Education exams usually taken at age 16 in Year 11 in England and Wales and Year 12 in Northern Ireland
Governors	people who are either appointed or elected to school governing bodies and have responsibility for overall governance, probity and management of a school
Highers/Advanced Highers	the main university entrance requirement for Scottish universities:

Highers are broadly equivalent to A levels in England, although most Scottish students will take four or five (at Secondary 5) to enter university;

Advanced Highers are optional but offer students (at Secondary 6) the opportunity to specialise or study a subject in greater depth to prepare them for direct entry to the second year of a four-year Scottish degree course

Glossary

HMI	Her Majesty's Inspectorate (of Schools): the non-ministerial government department that oversees the inspection regime of schools in England and runs Ofsted
HoD	head of department: the line-manager for the department, organising staffing, the syllabus of the subject and any exams related to it
IEP	Individual Education Plan: the specific aims and objectives set out for individual children with special educational needs
Independent school	A fee-paying, private school, often paradoxically known as a 'public school' because they were set up long before state or church provision at places like Eton, Rugby, Winchester and Westminster for 'public paupers', though that later changed to become largely the privileged public and the aristocracy.
Induction year	the probationary year, during which NQTs can expect additional support from an induction mentor and with a reduced teaching timetable to plan and prepare lessons
INSET	In-Service Education and Training: similar to CPD and usually referred to as training days at the beginning of term, these often take the form of some kind of in-school training delivered by an outside speaker
International school	privately funded, independent schools that cater for a mix of usually expatriate children and families in various parts of the world
ITT	Initial Teacher Training
KS	Key Stages 1, 2, 3, 4 and 5: the age-related stages of schooling in England, Wales and Northern Ireland, punctuated by tests (SATs) taken at the end of each
LA/LEA	local authority/local education authority

League tables	the ranking by which schools are compared according to the performance of their pupils in public examinations, either at Key Stage 2 SATs, GCSE and A Level
LSA	learning support assistant: teaching assistants who work in schools, usually to take small groups of children under the direction of a qualified teacher
Maintained/state sector	schools funded and governed either by local authorities or within academy status (in England)
MFL	modern foreign languages, usually referring to French, German and Spanish
NAHT	National Association of Head Teachers: a union
NASUWT	National Association of Schoolmasters Union of Women Teachers: one of the larger unions
National Curriculum	instituted by the Education Act of 1988, this provides "an entitlement to a broad and balanced education for all children" in England and Wales and includes both core and foundation subjects
NQT	newly qualified teacher, a term that indicates a teacher in their first year of work
NUT	National Union of Teachers: probably the largest union in the country
Ofsted	Office for Standards in Education: the government agency charged with inspecting schools in England
Peripatetic teachers	teachers who work, usually in a specialist role, in different schools on a part-time basis – often as music, instrumental, choir, foreign language or PE teachers (in primary education)
PGCE	Postgraduate Certificate of Education: the standard professional qualification for teaching in the UK

Glossary

PGDE	Postgraduate Diploma in Education (in Scotland)
PSHE	personal, social and health education: a foundation subject
PTA	parent–teacher association, a group of parents and teachers set up to support a school through various functions and fund-raising activities
Public school	an archaic term for an independent, privately run school in the UK, usually with charitable status
QTS	Qualified Teacher Status: the official, professionally recognised status of a fully qualified teacher in England, Wales and Northern Ireland
Role model	a person who sets an example for others to emulate
SATs	Standard Attainment Tests, (originally tasks) taken at ages 7, 11 and 14 in England and Northern Ireland and at 11 and 14 in Wales
SCITT	School-Centred Initial Teacher Training: the training of teachers in an employment-based setting, both primary and secondary, usually in collaboration with a local university to award QTS and often a PGCE
SEN	special educational needs: where children face particular and specific challenges in their learning, and where teachers and schools try to meet their needs with appropriate activities; specific needs might include social and behavioural needs, physical disabilities, autism and others
SENCO	special educational needs co-ordinator: the teacher responsible for managing the education plans for children on the school's SEN register
SLT/SMT	senior leadership team: a new name for senior management team; the team comprises the head teacher, deputy head and other senior teachers in the school

Special measures	the position a school is "placed in" if it "fails" an Ofsted inspection, meaning that the school is failing to supply an acceptable level of education and lacks the management and leadership capacity to improve. It also means that the school will be subject to regular short-notice inspections.
Special school	schools that cater for particular special educational needs, such as physical disabilities or social and emotional learning difficulties or autism
Supply teachers	teachers employed on a daily or short-term basis, usually to cover absence and within a contract determined by the agency employing them
TA	teaching assistant: someone who works under the direction of a qualified teacher and takes charge of small groups of children; some have training and qualifications, and in some schools are used to cover for teacher absence for limited periods
Teachers' Standards	the criteria set out by the Secretary of State for Education in England by which trainee teachers are judged in order to gain QTS, and against which their future competence and conduct can be bench-marked
TES	Times Educational Supplement
TQ	Teaching Qualification (in Scotland); similar to QTS in England
UCAS	Universities and Colleges Admissions Service for initial undergraduate and postgraduate enquiries for most teaching-training routes
Voice	formerly the Professional Association of Teachers (PAT) – a smaller (non-striking) union

Advertiser index